nourish

nourish

simon gault

photography KIERAN SCOTT

RANDOM HOUSE
NEW ZEALAND

contents

INTRODUCTION

SINCE MY TEENS, when I was an apprentice chef at Antoine's restaurant in Auckland, New Zealand, through the several years I spent cooking in Europe and around the world, and in all my restaurants, I have been and will remain a student of cooking.

From the time I could call a kitchen my own I adopted the same unbending and demanding attitude that was the norm during my training. I took a tough stand and was quite unfairly reported as being possessed of a singularly short fuse. Over the years my fuse has lengthened, but I remain committed to my original philosophy: that our guests should feel that we have surpassed their dining-experience expectations in every respect.

My role has also changed over the years. Now, as our businesses have grown, I find myself more and more playing the part of a conductor of a large 'orchestra' with my chefs as the players. Not only must I conduct them, I must also encourage the less experienced ones to hone their skills so as to blend in with others more accomplished and experienced. It became apparent to me very early on in this role that when a raised voice was used to enforce a view, the only person listening was the vocalist.

Within the New Zealand restaurant scene, I want to establish our restaurants as leaders and not followers. Most importantly, I want everyone in our teams to be proud of — and understand the importance of being part of — their particular restaurant.

An enormous amount of my time is now spent developing menu items and ideas that utilise the best available ingredients and present them in ways that lift and enhance their basic characteristics and flavours. To this end I travel whenever possible to see what my peers are doing. These journeys and visits to other kitchens enable me to introduce ideas that no amount of reading can supply. It is astonishing how complementary two entirely different cuisines can be; a mundane ingredient from one culture can be transformed into something extraordinary simply by the addition of an equally mundane ingredient taken from the food basics of a different culture.

In our Euro restaurant we focus on luxury ingredients: Alaskan king crab, caviar, whitebait and indeed any seasonal delicacies that we can source. At Pravda we have a smaller, less elaborate menu and we try to emulate the best aspects of home cooking. At the Jervois Steak House we source the very best steak possible; regrettably that is often not New Zealand grown. At Shed 5 we have our own fishmonger and fish-filleting room so we can do justice to the very best and freshest possible seafood. Sous Chef, our preferred supplier for imported ingredients, puts us in the happy position of having them find the best of what we want. This is an advantage that few chefs have and stems from our buying power. I take immense pleasure in these ventures and to have them all pulling together is extremely gratifying.

Within the pages of this book are recipes that reflect our desire to remain abreast of the latest food ideas and techniques. El Bulli in Spain, judged the finest restaurant in the world for the last three years, is open only six months of the year and is fully booked for the next few years. During the half-year that the restaurant is closed, the El Bulli workshop uses the time for research and development. This extraordinarily professional approach

has produced some of the most astonishing cooking aids imaginable. Within the Nourish Group, we have been quick to avail ourselves of the ingredients and tools to become part of the techno-inspired cuisine revolution. The recipes that make use of these ingredients and techniques may seem hardly worth the effort, but for the really committed chef they are too important to ignore. The few recipes presented here demonstrate only the basics of this new level in food presentation but they provide an insight into its potential.

On a personal level, the greatest pleasure for me when I am cooking is seeing the look of anticipatory delight on a diner's face when a dish is presented, followed by their body language as their first taste confirms the accuracy of the visual assessment. All chefs know that if a dish is not well presented the taste test becomes increasingly more difficult to pass. Food is always tasted first with the eyes, so if there is a way of making a dish look better, I want to know about it.

The recipes in this book are drawn in the main from the Nourish Group restaurant menus, along with some from earlier restaurants that I have owned. Interestingly, a few friends have questioned the wisdom of my giving away so many secrets here. For me, though, cooking is not about secrets; food is incredibly susceptible to the personality of the chef. Even if two chefs were to scrupulously follow the same ingredient list and method, the resulting two dishes would be significantly different. Serious chefs aim to delight and surprise the recipients of their work and, in doing so, their own preferences, personalities and prejudices are unconsciously added to the ingredient list. Is it any wonder that the end results would be so different?

I know there are many chefs who are technically better than I am, but my food is not only cooked with love but with the enjoyment of the diner as a priority. My hope is that *Nourish* will inspire others to try some of these dishes. Think of these recipes as a collection of ideas to get you headed in the right direction. With the wide choice of quality ingredients available from boutique stores — and even on occasion from the supermarket — the home cook can be far more confident and ambitious. I encourage you to search for the very best ingredients because a cheap alternative can wreck a dish, despite correct preparation. This kind of damage can be inflicted by a false sense of economy, for example using a cheap, vinegary, throat-gouging balsamic; a mistake made not solely by home cooks but also by many restaurant chefs. Searching for and buying the best products available gives any chef a massive advantage and — at the end of the day — this philosophy is in fact the most cost-effective. I appreciate that finding good-quality or more hard-to-find ingredients can be a little trying outside of the major cities, but after giving some thought to the 'feeling' of the dish, sensible, good-quality substitutes can often be made.

The recipes here represent ideas that hopefully will stimulate and encourage chefs (and home cooks) to progress them and create dishes suited to their own individual style. Remember that standing still is just another way of going backwards.

to begin

TOMATO TARTARE WITH BUFFALO MOZZARELLA, WITH OLIVE & ALMOND TRUFFLE CREAM & A PARMIGIANO CRISP

The appearance of this dish is deceptive in that although it is made from tomatoes it looks very like steak tartare topped with mozzarella di bufala. This chalk-white cheese is made from the milk of water buffalo farmed in Aversa in the province of Caserta, which is recognised as the original source of this famous Italian cheese. The mozzarella is soft, succulent and a real delicacy. The olive and almond truffle cream comes from Alba in the north of Italy, from the house of Tartufi Morra. During the season they buy in truffles on a daily basis and produce wonderful truffle products — from oils to pungent sauces; even truffle-flavoured salt. In my view, these truffle products are a pantry 'must have'. This olive and almond truffle cream, available from www.souschef.co.nz, spread sparingly on toasted ciabatta and topped with poached free-range eggs, makes for a sensational weekend breakfast.

300g vine-ripened tomatoes
20g capers, *finely chopped*
24g gherkins, *finely chopped*
30g shallots, *finely chopped*
2 tbsp tomato pesto
dash of Tabasco sauce
1 tbsp Worcestershire sauce
20g Dijon mustard
salt and pepper

tomato tartare

Prepare the tomatoes for skinning by first removing the cores, then cutting a cross in the other end of each tomato. Place in boiling water for about 1 minute or until the skin begins to curl away from the pulp at the cross cut. Remove and place in a container of iced water to stop the cooking process. When cool enough to handle, remove the skin, cut each tomato in half, then remove and discard the seeds. Dry the tomato flesh, then roughly chop and combine in a bowl with the capers, gherkins, shallots, tomato pesto, sauces and mustard. Mix to combine, then season with salt and pepper to taste. Place in a sieve and allow to sit over a bowl for 1 hour to allow excess liquid to drain off.

60g Parmigiano-Reggiano
  (do not substitute locally produced parmesan cheese)

parmigiano crisp

Finely grate the Parmigiano-Reggiano. Place a triangular cookie cutter on a flat plate or a baking tray. Fill the inside with the grated cheese, using only enough to form an even, thin layer; don't mound it up. Remove the cookie cutter and microwave the resulting triangular shape for 30–40 seconds. Allow to cool then, using a palette knife, lift the now-crisp cooked cheese and transfer it to an airtight container. Repeat the process to make six crisps. Store until required, but do not refrigerate.

Note: Any means of containing the grated cheese to form the desired shape for microwaving is acceptable, but an open-topped cookie cutter is probably the most convenient.

125g buffalo mozzarella cheese
6 sprigs of basil *(2 leaves each)*
3 tsp olive and almond truffle cream
  (optional)
2 tbsp Pukara extra-virgin olive oil
1 tbsp aged balsamic vinegar

special equipment 7cm diameter tube, cookie or pastry cutter

assembly

Place the tube on each serving plate in turn and spoon some tomato mixture into it, then lightly pack it down to a thickness of 1cm. Cut the mozzarella into six pieces and place one on top of each tartare along with a basil sprig and half a teaspoon of olive and almond truffle cream. Drizzle around each tartare 1 teaspoon of olive oil and half a teaspoon of aged balsamic. Finally, insert the parmigiano crisp, flag-style, into each tartare.

SERVES 6

TOMATO & BEET GAZPACHO MOUSSE ON LEMON CUCUMBER CARPACCIO WITH BUFFALO MOZZARELLA

Much uninformed comment is circulating at the time of writing relating to a dioxin risk from eating Italian buffalo mozzarella. As is often the case, the most outspoken of the doomsayers are the least informed. Of all the DOP cheeses in Italy, mozzarella di bufala is the most closely monitored throughout its phases of production. The consortium that oversees and regulates the production is the only organisation recognised by the Italian Ministry of Agriculture and Forestry Policies for the protection, surveillance, promotion and marketing of mozzarella di bufala campana cheese. We can be confident that no mozzarella di bufala that leaves Italy represents any sort of health risk.

60g acid-free tomatoes
40g Spanish red onion
1 medium clove garlic
¼ fresh red chilli
6g basil leaves
120g beetroot, *peeled and uncooked*
95g telegraph cucumber, *deseeded*
200ml tomato juice
1 tsp Tabasco chipotle pepper sauce
   (smoked)
1 tsp Worcestershire sauce
2g Murray River sea salt

beet gazpacho

Roughly chop all the ingredients, then place them in a stainless steel bowl. Cover and leave to marinate for 24 hours in the refrigerator.

Put the gazpacho ingredients in a blender and process until smooth, then pass through a sieve to remove any lumps. Set aside.

200ml beet gazpacho *(see above)*
2 leaves gelatine, *soaked in cold water*
   to soften
10 slices white toast bread, *crusts removed*

gazpacho mousse

Heat 100ml of the beet gazpacho mix in a heavy saucepan. Remove the gelatine from the water and squeeze dry. Add the softened leaves of gelatine to the heated gazpacho and stir to dissolve, then mix in the remaining 100ml of gazpacho to cool the mix.

Blend the bread and the gazpacho and gelatine mix in a blender or food processor until smooth. Pour into a bowl. Cover and refrigerate for 2 hours.

200ml olive oil
12 basil leaves

fried basil

Heat the olive oil in a heavy-bottomed 20cm pan to 165°C. Place the dry basil leaves into the heated oil, taking care to avoid hot oil splattering. Cook the leaves for about 20–30 seconds without colouring, as this will make them taste bitter. Once crisp, remove the leaves from the oil and place on a paper towel to absorb the excess oil.

1 telegraph cucumber, *unpeeled*
250g buffalo mozzarella, *cut into 6 pieces*
2 tbsp lemon juice
2 tbsp Pukara extra-virgin olive oil
2 tbsp Prelibato white balsamic vinegar
Murray River sea salt
9 grissini sticks *(see page 186)*

assembly

Using a sharp knife, cut the cucumber into 60 thin slices. Use them to make an overlapping circle on each plate. In the centre of the cucumber circle, place two scoops of the gazpacho mousse with a piece of mozzarella on the side. Drizzle each plate with 1 teaspoon of lemon juice, 1 teaspoon of olive oil, 1 teaspoon of Prelibato white balsamic vinegar and a sprinkle of Murray River sea salt. Garnish with two fried basil leaves, and one and a half grissini sticks.

SERVES 6

LEMON & PRAWN ARANCINI ON WILTED SPINACH WITH WARM MANDARIN-PEPPER JELLY

Arancini (which in Italian means 'little oranges') are tasty balls of rice coated in the style of schnitzel, but deep-fried instead of pan-fried. Making these are an excellent way of using up any excess risotto and they are elegant snacks or antipasti. They are best eaten just after being made; the mozzarella in the centre of the arancini comes as a melting surprise. The prawn can be substituted for crab, lobster or mussels. I prefer to make them small enough to be suitable for finger food, which can still be attractive as a light meal by adding one or two additional arancini to each serving. Preparing the rice especially for the dish is certainly worth the effort. If you have Texturas Gellan the warm jelly is fantastic; otherwise, use the recipe for cold jelly.

500ml fish or clam stock
50g butter
2 tbsp Pukara extra-virgin olive oil
½ medium onion, *finely diced*
2 cloves garlic, minced
¾ cup (140g) Arborio rice
100ml white wine
zest of 1 lemon
150g prawn meat, *roughly diced*
40g Parmigiano-Reggiano
1 tbsp chopped parsley
salt and pepper
60g buffalo mozzarella cheese, *cut into 18 small pieces*
½ cup plain flour
4 eggs, *lightly beaten*
2½ cups breadcrumbs
about 1 litre canola oil

risotto

To make the risotto, combine the stock and butter in a saucepan and bring to the boil. Turn off the heat. In a separate, 1.5 litre saucepan, heat the olive oil and sauté the onion and garlic on a low heat until transparent. Add the rice and sauté for 3 minutes, stirring continuously with a wooden spoon. Add the white wine and stir over a medium heat until the rice absorbs the wine. Then add half a cup of hot butter stock, stirring to ensure it does not catch. When it has been absorbed, add the lemon zest and continue adding the stock, half a cup at a time, until the stock and butter have been absorbed. When adding the last half cup of stock and the last knob of butter, add the chopped prawns. The process should take 25–35 minutes and the rice should be al dente. Add the cheese and chopped parsley. Season with salt and pepper. Spread the risotto onto a tray and leave it to cool.

arancini

When cool, divide the risotto into six portions, then further divide each portion into three and roll into small balls so that you have a total of 18. Take each ball and flatten one side, making an indentation in the centre. Place a piece of mozzarella into the hole, then seal well. Repeat with all 18 balls. Roll each in flour, then dip into the beaten egg to coat well. Roll the balls in the breadcrumbs, pressing breadcrumbs into any uncovered areas.

Place enough canola oil in a saucepan to ensure the balls will be covered in oil while frying. Heat the oil to 185°C. Fry the balls in batches until they are golden brown and hot in the middle. Drain on paper towels. They can be reheated in the oven.

SIMON SAYS *If you don't have an oil thermometer, test the temperature of the oil by dropping in a 5cm square of white bread and timing to see how long it takes to turn golden brown; it should take 50 seconds.*

½ small red chilli, *deseeded*
350ml mandarin juice
6g Texturas Gellan (for hot jellies) or
   3 leaves gelatine (for cold jellies)

mandarin-pepper jelly

If making the hot jelly, finely chop the chilli and divide it equally between the six moulds. Set the moulds aside. Place the mandarin juice into a saucepan with the Gellan. Bring to the boil and simmer for 30 seconds. Strain the juice, then pour equal quantities onto the chilli in each of the moulds. Allow to set; this should only take about 5 minutes.

If making the cold jelly, finely chop the chilli and divide it equally between the six moulds. Set the moulds aside. Soak the gelatine leaves in a bowl of cold water. Place the mandarin juice in a saucepan, bring to the boil and simmer for 1 minute. Add the softened gelatine leaves and stir until they dissolve. Remove from the heat and strain. Divide the juice equally between the six moulds. Place in the refrigerator to set.

wilted spinach

250g spinach, *washed and picked*
2 tbsp Pukara extra-virgin olive oil
1 tbsp butter
salt and pepper

special equipment 6 x 30ml moulds

Heat the oil and butter in a sauté pan, add the spinach and sauté until wilted. Season with salt and pepper.

assembly

If you are serving hot jellies, reheat them in a preheated 150°C oven for 4 minutes.

Divide the spinach and arancini balls between six plates. Turn out the hot jellies, one on each plate, and serve. If you are serving cold jellies, follow the same instructions for serving but do not reheat the jellies.

SERVES 6

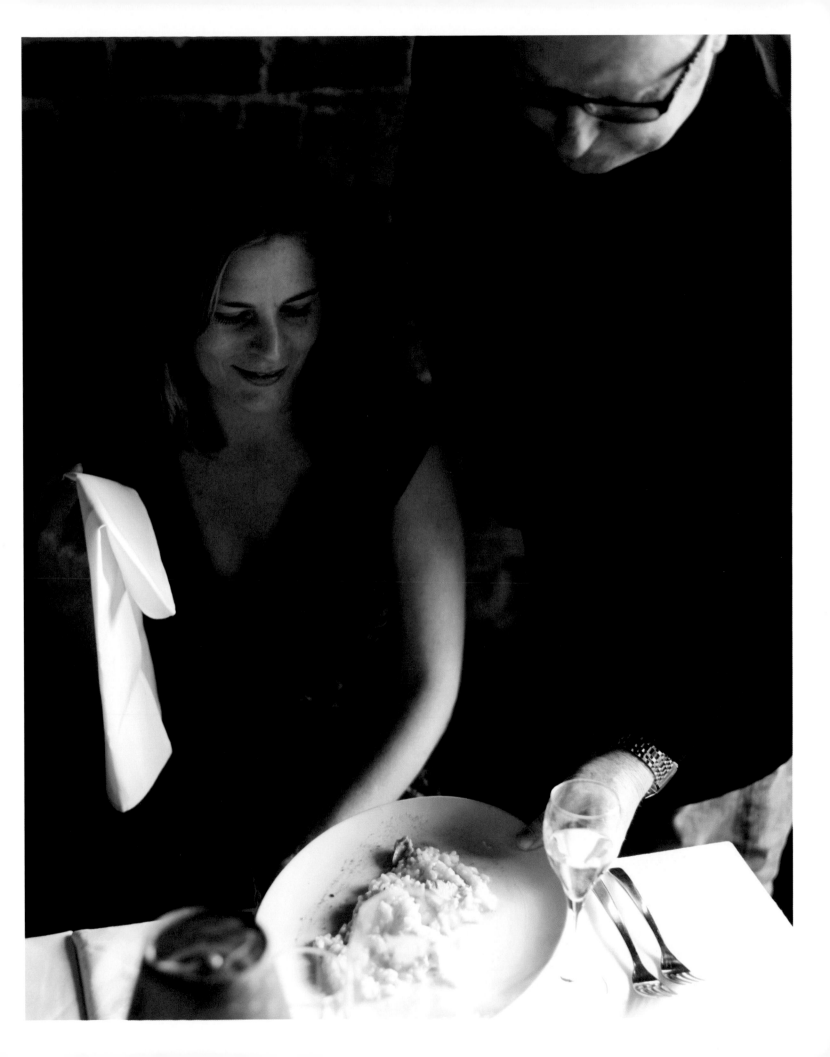

SHISO TARTARE OF TUNA WITH WASABI CAVIAR & BEET JUICE DRESSING & PINE NUTS

I imagine that many people's introduction to tuna has been via a can, but unless heavily disguised with some more acceptable ingredients I find the flavour of canned tuna to be reminiscent of low-grade cardboard. Fresh tuna is completely different and superb to work with, immensely versatile — and delicious, as the Japanese discovered long ago. Unlike most fish species, which have white flesh, tuna have pink to dark red flesh. There are also several species that are warm blooded. Tuna is very high in protein and low in fat and is equally appetising served cooked or uncooked. The sashimi grade of tuna called for in the tartare ingredients indicates that it is top grade and the recipe really does warrant this quality.

550g sashimi-grade yellowfin tuna
100ml wasabi vinaigrette *(see below)*
120g shiso leaf *(available from Japanese food stores), finely diced*
90g spring onion, *finely diced*
140g wasabi tobiko caviar
salt *(optional)*

150ml vinaigrette *(see page 233)*
50ml mirin
20ml soy sauce
1 tsp wasabi powder

150g mascarpone
40g wasabi tobiko caviar
1 tbsp finely diced spring onion
½ tsp salt
pinch of white pepper

300ml water
75g caster sugar
1 litre still mineral water
3.2g Texturas Algin
1 medium beetroot
½ tbsp wasabi powder
1 tbsp Texturas Gluco
30 pine nuts

tartare
With a sharp knife, cut the tuna into approximately 2mm brunoise. Place in a bowl and keep covered in the refrigerator until ready to assemble. Just prior to assembly, add wasabi vinaigrette, the shiso leaf, spring onion and 120g of the caviar, reserving the rest for garnish. Mix well with a fork. Taste and add salt if desired.

wasabi vinaigrette
Whisk the ingredients in a bowl. Set aside.

wasabi mascarpone
In a bowl, mix the ingredients together with a wooden spoon. Cover and refrigerate.

beetroot sphere
In a saucepan, combine the first measure of water with the caster sugar and bring to the boil. Simmer for 2 minutes, then allow the sugar syrup to cool. Pour 500ml of the mineral water into a blender and add the Algin. Blend for 3–6 seconds or until the Algin is incorporated. Pour into a small container and set aside. Place the remaining 500ml in a separate container.

Place the beetroot in a saucepan. Cover with water and bring to the boil. Simmer, keeping covered with water, until the beetroot is just past tender. Run the beetroot under cold water, rubbing off the skin. Remove the top and tail along with any fibrous root or stem material. Roughly chop the cooked beetroot and place in a measuring jug. Pour the cooled sugar syrup over the beetroot to reach the 250ml level on the side of the jug. Discard any remaining syrup.

Transfer the beetroot and syrup along with the wasabi powder to a blender and process until a fine purée is achieved. Allow to cool. Add the

Gluco to the cold beetroot purée and blend for a further 20 seconds. Pass through a sieve and set aside in the refrigerator until ready to assemble.

Place the pine nuts in a sauté pan over a low heat, moving the pan continuously to achieve a golden colour. Turn out on to a cold tray to stop further colouring. Fill a tablespoon measure with beetroot purée, add five pine nuts and gently pour into the mineral water and algin mixture to form a sphere. Allow the sphere to consolidate for 3 minutes before removing with a slotted or draining spoon and immediately rinse in the reserved mineral water while still on the spoon. Transfer the rinsed sphere to another spoon until you are ready to place it on the tartare. Repeat the process to make six spheres.

assembly
Place the tube on a serving plate and insert a serving of tuna. Pack it down inside, leaving a 3mm space. Add the wasabi mascarpone mix, and smooth the top with a palette knife. Using a thin knife, loosen the mixture around the edges and remove the contents from the tube onto the plate. Repeat to make six servings. Pour 45ml (3 tbsp) of wasabi vinaigrette around each plate and garnish the vinaigrette with the remaining caviar. Place a beetroot sphere on top of each tartare and serve.

SERVES 6

special equipment *5cm tube, cylinder or pastry cutter*

TUNA LINE WITH JALAPEÑO MELON CAVIAR & APPLE & RICOTTA SALAD

This is my take on sashimi, which I concede does not conform to the sashimi served in most Japanese restaurants but nevertheless has been known to make a grown Japanese man cry (I had no idea that these inscrutable gentlemen had such emotional fragility). The jalapeño melon caviar puts this dish in the 'molecular gastronomy' category and utilises the magical aids developed by the El Bulli Workshop in Spain. If you do not have access to Texturas Algin and Calcic, replace the jalapeño melon caviar with salmon caviar. Very fresh sashimi-grade tuna is essential for this recipe.

500g tuna, *cut from the centre of a small loin, about 21cm long*

tuna
Place the tuna on a clean cutting board. Using a sharp knife, slice the fish in half lengthways, then cut each half into three equal lengths to yield six portions. Transfer to a plate and cover with cling film. Refrigerate until 30 minutes prior to assembly, when it must be brought close to room temperature.

½ ripe rock melon
1 tbsp Tabasco green pepper sauce (Jalapeño)
sugar syrup *(see page 232)*
1.6g Texturas Algin
1 litre still mineral water
3.5g Texturas Calcic

jalapeño melon caviar
Deseed the rock melon. Spoon the flesh into a blender and purée to a juice. Push through a fine mesh sieve and add the Tabasco sauce and enough sugar syrup as necessary to achieve 250ml. Pour the juice mixture back into a high-speed blender and add the Algin. Blend at high speed for 20 seconds. Pour the mixture into a clean container and refrigerate for at least 2 hours to allow all the air in the juice to escape.

Rinse the blender jug and pour in 500ml of the mineral water. Add the Calcic, blend on high speed for 20 seconds, then pour into a medium-sized bowl and leave to rest for at least 2 hours.

Make the melon caviar next. Load the syringe (included in the Texturas tool kit) with the melon mixture. Carefully drop the melon mixture, one drop at a time, into the Calcic solution. The droplets will set into small balls resembling caviar. Leave the droplets in the solution for 3 minutes and then lift out using a slotted spoon. Rinse the balls in 250ml of the mineral water and store in a small bowl covered with the rest of the mineral water.

2 Granny Smith apples
60g ricotta cheese

apple and ricotta salad
Peel and cut the apples into fine brunoise. Do this just before assembly so that the apple remains fresh and crisp and does not begin to go brown. Have the ricotta in a bowl ready to go, along with the remaining ingredients.

salt and pepper
3 tsp Pukara extra-virgin olive oil
6 tbsp apple syrup
6 tsp Pukara extra-virgin olive oil
12 tsp apple balsamic vinegar
    (or substitute a good-quality aged balsamic vinegar)
1 small packet micro greens to garnish

special equipment *1 basic spherification kit, Texturas tool kit*

assembly
Place each tuna strip on a suitable plate and lightly season with salt and pepper. Drizzle with half a teaspoon of extra-virgin olive oil and 1 tablespoon of apple syrup. Divide the ricotta cheese into 6 portions and sprinkle one portion over the length of each tuna strip. Repeat with the apple and then drizzle each serving with 1 teaspoon of extra virgin olive oil and 2 teaspoons of apple balsamic vinegar. Top with a few micro greens. Finish with the jalapeño melon caviar scattered over the dish. Serve immediately.

ALASKAN CRAB CANNELLONI WITH CHILLI MELON RELISH

Cannelloni was invented in 1907 at 'O Parrucchiano restaurant in Sorrento, Italy, by the chef Salvatore Coletta. A woman called Luisella Romano, who worked at 'O Parrucchiano for 70 years until she passed away at the age of 90, exclusively prepared the tomatoes for the cannelloni sauce. At the time of her death Luisella had nearly perfected it.

These cannelloni do not use Luisella's famous sauce nor is it pasta wrapping; the following recipe's only similarity is the shape. My reason for introducing the term cannelloni was really just an excuse to tell you about Luisella. This recipe makes great finger food or a lunch and it is gluten free.

360g Alaskan crab meat *(shell-inclusive weight 700g)*
5 tbsp mayonnaise *(see page 232)*
2 tbsp chives, *finely chopped*
15 g wasabi tobiko caviar
juice of ½ lemon
1 tsp Tabasco green pepper sauce *(Jalapeño)*
salt
6 x 22cm rice paper wrappers *(available from Asian food markets)*

crab cannelloni

In a bowl, mix together the crab meat, mayonnaise, chives, caviar, lemon juice and Tabasco. Season with salt to taste. To prepare the rice paper wrappers, pour enough boiling water into a shallow dish to reach 2cm. Submerge the wrappers in the water until they become translucent and soft (about 20 seconds). Place the wrappers on a clean tea towel to dry off any excess water.

Spoon 2 heaped tablespoons of crab-meat mixture in a line down the middle of each wrapper. Fold in the ends to contain the mixture and roll up. This may take several attempts to get right but is very easy and quick once you have the knack. Place the finished rice paper rolls on a plate covered with a damp tea towel to keep them from drying out.

½ rock melon
1 tsp finely chopped mild chilli
1 tbsp finely chopped coriander
1 tbsp Pukara extra-virgin olive oil
2 tsp Prelibato white balsamic vinegar
pinch of salt

melon relish

Remove the skin and seeds from the melon and discard. Finely dice the flesh. Place in a bowl and add the chilli, coriander, olive oil, balsamic and salt and mix together.

2 tbsp Pukara extra-virgin olive oil
6 Alaskan crab claws or leg pieces
1 tsp finely chopped chives
10g wasabi tobiko caviar

assembly

Place three small piles of melon relish on each plate. Diagonally slice each rice paper roll into three pieces and place one on each pile of relish. Drizzle with the extra-virgin olive oil and place a crab leg or claw on each plate. Sprinkle with the chopped chives and share the caviar over the cannelloni.

SERVES 6

ALASKAN CRAB WITH FRIED WEST COAST WHITEBAIT, OSCIÈTRE CAVIAR BUTTER & ALBA TRUFFLE

My first experience of Alaskan crab was in Alaska while working on Larry Ellison's motor yacht Ronin. We were adopted by a local fisherman who quickly realised how to keep his bread buttered. He would follow us around, waiting for us to call him on the radio to find out what delicacy he had sourced for us. This extravagant but superb dish originated from that entrepreneurial association. Even if the budget denies the inclusion of the truffle and caviar, it is still a very impressive dish. The butter sauce is just wonderful drizzled over any seafood and substituting six crushed green peppercorns for the caviar makes it eminently suitable as a sauce for chicken or steak.

osciètre caviar butter

80ml white wine
25g shallots, *finely diced*
40ml white wine vinegar
1 bay leaf
1 small clove garlic, *minced*
8 black peppercorns
200ml cream
80g cold unsalted butter, *diced*
salt

Put the wine, shallots, vinegar, bay leaf, garlic and peppercorns into a small saucepan. Bring to the boil and simmer slowly for 3–4 minutes or until reduced to approximately 1 tablespoon. Add the cream, return to a simmer and reduce by half or until starting to thicken (if reduced too much the cream will split). Lower the heat so that the mixture is no longer simmering and whisk in the cold butter, piece by piece. After half the butter cubes have been stirred in, they can be added two at a time. Continue stirring until all the butter has been added and the sauce thickens. Do not allow the sauce to boil at any time. Add salt to taste at the end. Strain into a flask (discarding the shallot, bay leaves, garlic and peppercorns) and keep warm until ready to use. The flask can be placed in warm water to maintain the temperature and prevent the butter from congealing.

crab

6 medium Alaskan red king crab legs
1 tbsp canola oil

Preheat the oven to 180°C. Carefully remove the crab meat from the shells, ensuring it comes out in one piece. This is not usually difficult: crab shells are soft and a sharp pair of scissors make light work of the task. Lay the crab meat on an oven tray greased with the canola oil, then cover with tin foil. Place the covered crab in the oven for 4 minutes.

SIMON SAYS *When pulling out the crab flesh, pull it away from the claw tip; it will come out more cleanly and is less inclined to break up.*

whitebait

200ml canola oil
150g whitebait
50g flour, *seasoned with salt and pepper*

While the crab is heating, prepare the whitebait. In a sauté pan, heat the canola oil to a shimmer. Dust the whitebait in the seasoned flour and sauté until crispy (approximately 30 seconds). Remove the whitebait from the oil and drain on paper towels.

assembly

6g osciètre caviar
Alba black truffle, *thinly sliced*

Stir the caviar into the butter sauce. Place some hot crab on each plate and pour over the caviar sauce. Top with a few whitebait and garnish with a little thinly sliced black truffle.

SERVES 6

SCALLOPS ON PRAWN BRANDADE WITH CARROT & GINGER BUTTER FOAM

Brandade is a dish served in the south of France. It usually consists of salt cod, olive oil, milk or thick cream and garlic. While this combination of ingredients may not sound particularly appetising, it is delicious and one of my all-time favourites. This brandade can also be used as a dip for crostini or raw carrot and/or celery.

1 cup rock salt
350g cod fillets
150g raw prawn meat, *diced*
200ml Pukara extra-virgin olive oil
1 medium white onion, *finely diced*
1 medium clove garlic, *minced*
750ml milk
pinch of nutmeg
¼ tsp white pepper

prawn brandade

Sprinkle half the rock salt evenly over a platter just big enough to hold the fish fillets. Place the cod on top, then sprinkle over the remaining salt. Cover and refrigerate for a minimum of 8 hours. Uncover and rinse well under cold running water, then place in a bowl and cover with water and allow to soak, refrigerated, for 2 hours. After this time, drain off the water and repeat the process with fresh water for a further 3 hours. The longer the fish is soaked, the less likely the end dish will be over-salty. Drain the fillets and run under cold water, then pat dry with paper towels.

Cook the prawn meat in boiling salted water. Use 1 tablespoon of salt per litre of water. Drain and set aside.

Sauté the onion and garlic in half the olive oil (100ml) until translucent then add the cod. Flake and stir the fish with a wooden spoon over a medium heat for 3 minutes. Continue to stir and add half the milk, 50ml at a time, then stir in the remaining 100ml of oil. Slowly stir in the remaining milk to achieve a flaky mashed potato consistency. Add the nutmeg and pepper and adjust the seasoning if necessary. Add the cooked prawn meat and set aside.

1 tbsp Pukara extra-virgin olive oil
100g shallots, *finely chopped*
4 medium cloves garlic, *minced*
60ml Stones green ginger wine
50g fresh ginger, *peeled and grated*
300g carrots, *cooked until soft*
250ml cream
1½ tsp salt
pinch of white pepper

carrot and ginger foam

In a medium-sized saucepan, heat the olive oil and sauté the shallots and garlic until translucent; take care not to colour them. Add the green ginger wine, ginger and carrots, bring to the boil and simmer for 2 minutes. Add the cream, salt and pepper and bring back to the boil. Simmer for 4 minutes, then remove from the heat and process in a blender to a smooth consistency. Pass through a fine sieve. For sauce of the lightest consistency, load into a whipped cream dispenser. Alternatively, simply spoon the sauce over when serving.

18 medium scallops for a starter
  or 36 for a main course
salt and pepper
1 tbsp Pukara extra-virgin olive oil
25g butter

scallops

Make sure the scallops are thoroughly dry before cooking. Season with salt and pepper. Heat the olive oil to a shimmer in a sauté pan and add the butter, followed by the seasoned scallops. Sauté until they firm up and are hot in the middle (about 30 seconds). Take care not to overcook them or they will become tough and rubbery.

6 sprigs chervil

assembly

Reheat the prawn brandade and divide equally between six plates. Divide the scallops and place on top, finishing with some carrot and ginger foam. Garnish with a sprig of chervil.

special equipment *whipped cream dispenser*

SERVES 6

CALAMARI SCHNITZEL WITH PARSLEY, TOASTED CAPERS & LEMON

*This dish evolved over time out of my determination to present a melt-in-the-mouth calamari steak.
I desperately wanted to present a seafood alternative at the Jervois Steak House and while I liked the idea
of calamari, I did not want to risk the inconsistency in tenderness that is so often its downfall. However, this
recipe has worked well for me and is a valuable one to add to a home kitchen arsenal. The pre-prepared
schnitzels will keep well in the freezer and are a show-stopper for that unexpected dinner party. Allow
45 minutes for the schnitzels to defrost before you sauté them, then serve with the flair one associates with
a chef who has dreamt up a last-minute masterpiece.*

schnitzel

5 leaves gelatine
600g squid tubes
½ tbsp salt
1 tsp white pepper
1 tsp fish stock powder
1 cup flour
3 eggs, lightly beaten
2 cups breadcrumbs
90ml Pukara extra-virgin olive oil
3 tbsp butter

Soak the gelatine leaves in some cold water until soft. While they are soaking, slice the calamari into strips, then transfer to a food processor. Purée until it forms a smooth paste; this will take a few minutes. Stop the machine every 30 seconds and scrape the sides down to the blade to ensure every scrap is processed smoothly. Add the salt, pepper and fish stock powder to the processor. Drain the water from the gelatine, drop into a small pan over a low heat and melt down to a liquid. Add the liquid gelatine to the calamari paste and purée for 1 minute. Transfer the mixture to a bowl and divide into six equal portions. Using a palette knife and working on a sheet of baking paper, shape each portion into a 5mm-thick schnitzel shape. Freeze the schnitzels on a tray so that they remain perfectly flat.

When the schnitzels are frozen, place the flour, beaten egg and breadcrumbs into three separate bowls or trays that are large enough to accommodate the frozen schnitzels one at a time. Place each schnitzel in the flour, then in the egg and finally into the breadcrumbs, ensuring they are completely coated. Store in the refrigerator or freezer, depending on how soon they will be required. Make sure they are wrapped tightly in cling film, particularly if they are to be retained frozen.

capers

100ml canola oil
36 capers

Heat the canola oil to a shimmer in a sauté pan and fry the capers until they become crispy. Remove and drain on paper towels.

assembly

6 tbsp mayonnaise *(see page 232)*
1 small clove garlic, *very finely chopped*
1 tbsp Pukara extra-virgin olive oil
½ tbsp butter
6 lemon wedges
1 tbsp chopped parsley

Mix the mayonnaise and garlic together and place in a small plastic squeeze bottle. Set aside. Preheat the oven to 100°C. Heat extra-virgin olive oil and butter in a sauté pan. When the butter and oil mix is bubbling, place a calamari schnitzel in the pan and cook over a medium heat until golden brown underneath. Flip and cook the other side. Turn down the heat to low and cook for a further 3 minutes. Remove and keep hot in the oven until the remaining schnitzels are ready. Garnish each plate with some garlic mayonnaise, then place a schnitzel on top. Add a wedge of lemon and sprinkle with the fried capers and parsley.

SERVES 6

ALASKAN KING CRAB & PRAWN IN JALAPEÑO CRÈME FRAÎCHE SAUCE TOPPED WITH TUNA WAFERS

If you have never seen tuna wafers served on a hot dish, this is a real show-stopper. The dish is delicious in its own right but the entertainment value of the tuna wafers — which begin moving and thus appear alive — takes it into the realm of the comedy kitchen.

240g picked Alaskan red king crab meat
660g crème fraîche
2½ tablespoons Jalapeño Tabasco sauce
100g wasabi tobiko caviar
salt
240g prawn meat, *chopped*
20g dried bonito tuna flakes *(available from Japanese food stores)*

Preheat the oven to 180°C. Check there is no shell or cartilage in the crab meat. Mix the crème fraîche with the Tabasco sauce and half the wasabi tobiko caviar, and season with salt. Divide the prawn meat, crab meat and the crème fraîche mixture between six small ovenproof dishes. Place in the oven for 7 minutes or until hot and bubbling. To serve, divide the remaining wasabi caviar and sprinkle over each dish, then sprinkle the bonito tuna flakes evenly over the dishes. Serve hot, straight from the oven.

SERVES 6

TERRINE OF OXTAIL & FOIE GRAS WITH A SAUTERNES & GREEN PEPPERCORN JELLY WITH CRISPY BRUSCHETTA

A terrine is by definition an oblong or oval cooking dish with vertical sides and a close-fitting lid. But it has, over time, come to refer to the food prepared in it. If the contents are pressed and turned out to slice for serving, as in this recipe, it becomes a pâté. Pâté of oxtail did not convey the intended personality of this dish, so I say it's a terrine and the purists can take a hike.

2 large carrots, *about 150g*
1 medium onion
3 stalks celery
10 cloves garlic
4 tbsp Pukara extra-virgin olive oil
2kg oxtail pieces
salt and pepper
8 cups chicken stock
100g can foie gras
8g toasted pine nuts

terrine

Preheat the oven to 180°C. Peel both carrots, reserve one, peel the onion and wash the celery, then cut all but the reserved carrot into rough 2cm dice. Crush the garlic cloves with the back of a knife. Heat half the olive oil in a large saucepan and add the chopped vegetables and garlic. Sauté over a medium to high heat until lightly browned. Transfer to a large ovenproof dish and set aside.

Use a paper towel to wipe the pan clean, then add the remaining oil and increase the heat to high. Lightly season the oxtail pieces with the salt and pepper. Using tongs, place the largest pieces of the oxtail into the pan and brown on all sides. Transfer the browned meat to the vegetables and repeat with the smaller pieces. Pour the chicken stock over and cover the dish with a tight-fitting lid or tin foil. Place in the oven and cook for 2 ½–3 hours until the meat falls from the bones. Leave to cool in the cooking liquid.

When cool enough to handle, skim as much fat as possible from the surface and pull the meat from the bones and shred. Discard any remaining fat and bone. Strain the liquid into a saucepan and skim off all the remaining fat. Reduce over a medium heat until just 60ml of intensely flavoured jus remains. Pour the jus over the oxtail and mix. Season with salt and white pepper. Take the remaining carrot and trim off one side to create a flat edge. Roll the carrot onto the flat side and trim off the rounded edge to create a rectangular carrot with four flat sides. Slice the squared carrot lengthways to achieve four equal carrot batons. Blanch the batons in boiling salted water for 1½ minutes and then place into iced water to cool.

Line the terrine mould with a double layer of cling film, pressing well into the corners of the mould and making sure there is plenty of cling film hanging over the sides. Press about one-third of the cooked oxtail meat into the terrine mould. Spread half the foie gras over the top of the oxtail and sprinkle with half the pine nuts, then arrange the carrot batons on top so they run in two lines end to end down the middle. Make a second layer on top of the carrot batons with half the remaining oxtail meat, topping with the rest of the foie gras. Use the last of the oxtail meat to cover, then pull the overhanging cling film over the top of the terrine, smoothing it down to seal. Turn the mould upside down on a flat board or plate and refrigerate overnight to set.

90ml sauternes
30g sugar
2 tbsp cold water
1 leaf gelatine or 2g powdered gelatine
1 tsp crushed green peppercorns

sauternes jelly

Pour the sauternes into a clean saucepan and add the sugar and water. In a small container, cover the gelatine with water and allow to soften (if using powdered gelatine, mix 1 tablespoon of water with the powdered gelatine for 1 minute). Bring the contents of the saucepan to the boil and simmer gently for 1½ minutes. Add the crushed peppercorns, take off the heat and whisk in the gelatine. Leave to infuse for 5 minutes, then strain through a fine mesh strainer into a square-sided container and refrigerate to set. This should take about 1 hour. Cut the jelly into six equal portions using a small pastry cutter or a teaspoon.

18 slices ciabatta bread
3 tbsp Pukara extra-virgin olive oil
1 clove garlic

bruschetta

Preheat the oven to 180°C. Using a pastry brush, lightly brush the bread on both sides with the olive oil and place in a single layer on an oven tray. Bake until golden and crispy (about 5 minutes). Remove from the oven and when cool enough to handle, rub each side lightly with the cut garlic clove. Once at room temperature, the bruschetta can be stored in an airtight container ready for use.

special equipment *terrine mould 27.5cm long x 4cm wide x 5.5cm deep*

assembly

Preheat the oven to 180°C. Place the bruschetta on an oven tray and place in the oven for 1 minute to warm through. Remove the terrine from the mould, discarding the cling film. Using a sharp knife, slice the terrine into 24 x 1cm thick slices. Arrange four slices per person on a suitable plate alongside the jelly and the warm bruschetta.

SIMON SAYS *Serve with some salt flakes and crushed green peppercorns.*

SERVES 6

COS LETTUCE SALAD WITH CAESAR AïOLI, BLACK TRUFFLE MUSHROOM PASTE, CORN POWDER & TEMPURA EGG YOLK

Some years ago, when Caesar salads were fairly new to the New Zealand restaurant scene, I wanted to grab the attention of guests in one of my early restaurants so I began serving my salads in highly polished Volkswagen hub caps. I didn't sell many Volkswagens, but I sure sold a lot of salads. Nowadays restaurants have many variations of the traditional Caesar on their menus. I, too, have moved on to incorporate innovations but the basic ingredients remain true to tradition. This salad recipe includes subtle additional flavours that in my view enhance what has become an enduring favourite. When serving it, encourage the diner to mix all the ingredients together but only after allowing their eye to savour the presentation and advise the taste buds that something special is on the way.

corn powder *(must be made 14 hours in advance)*

330g can corn kernels
160ml water
½ tbsp salt

Drain off half the liquid from the canned corn. Pour the remaining liquid and the corn kernels into a Pacojet beaker (see page 235). Add the water and salt, then freeze overnight. Pacotise the entire beaker, then refreeze. When required, pacotise one portion at a time to make powder and keep in the freezer.

salad

½ large cos lettuce
60g streaky bacon

Preheat the oven to 180°C. Remove and discard the large outer leaves of the cos lettuce, along with any that are broken or bruised. Cut off the base and discard, then wash the leaves in cold water and dry thoroughly. Keep refrigerated until ready to assemble. Roughly chop the bacon, place on an oven tray and bake for 8 minutes. Transfer the bacon onto paper towels to drain off excess fat.

Caesar aïoli

2 egg yolks
5 anchovy fillets
½ small clove garlic
1 tbsp lemon juice
1 tsp Worcestershire sauce
1 tsp Dijon mustard
1½ tbsp Parmigiano-Reggiano cheese
100ml canola oil and 50ml Pukara extra-virgin olive oil, *combined*
4 tbsp mayonnaise *(see page 232)*

Place all the ingredients except for the oils and mayonnaise in a food processor and process to a paste. Transfer to a mixing bowl. In a steady stream, but very slowly, trickle in the oils, a little at a time, while whisking so that the dressing becomes thick and glossy. Finally add the mayonnaise.

tempura egg yolk

400ml canola oil
6 eggs
50g flour
200ml tempura batter *(see page 233)*

Preheat the oil in a saucepan until it reaches 185°C. Separate each egg yolk from its white, one at a time. Place the flour in a shallow bowl and roll each yolk very carefully in the flour so that the yolk has a nice thin layer of flour around it. Tilt the flour container to aid the rolling and to protect the egg yolk. Carefully lift out the yolk and ease it into the tempura batter. Using a slotted spoon, lift the yolk out of the batter and roll off the spoon into the hot oil. Cook for 45 seconds, then remove from the oil and drain on a paper towel. Repeat with the rest of the egg yolks.

6 tbsp black trumpet mushroom truffle
   paste *(see page 239 Crema Con Tartufo)*
70g croutons *(see page 231)*

special equipment *Pacojet*

assembly

Cut the larger lettuce leaves in half lengthways, reserving the small
leaves. Stack the large leaves on top of each other, then chop them into
bite-sized pieces. Transfer all the lettuce, including the small leaves, to a
mixing bowl. Add 3 tablespoons of the Caesar aïoli, the bacon and the
croutons and mix together. Build a small salad on each plate, making sure
the bacon and croutons are evenly distributed. To one side of salad add
1 tablespoon of the mushroom truffle paste. On the other side of the
salad put 1 teaspoon of Caesar aïoli and sit the tempura egg yolk on this.
Finish the plate with 1 tablespoon of the frozen corn powder, positioned
to balance the presentation. Serve immediately.

SIMON SAYS *If you do not have a Pacojet you will not be able to make
the corn powder. However, the dish remains very tasty without this
embellishment.*

SERVES 6

ARTICHOKE, PRESERVED LEMON, ROCKET & CHÈVRE WRAPPED IN SERRANO HAM

Globe artichokes were first cultivated in Italy around Naples in the middle of the ninth century. I still use the Italian variety because of the absence of the inedible 'choke', the immature floret in the centre of the flower bud. The canned artichokes used for this recipe are the bud and part of the stem — both of which are edible and tender. The company in Italy that cans these artichokes is Menù. Presented in lightly herbed oil this product is available from some of the better delicatessens.

3 whole cooked artichokes with stem
¼ salt-preserved lemon *(optional)*
13 whole walnuts
60g rocket *(arugula)*
30ml olive oil
30ml white balsamic vinegar
6 slices Serrano ham
120g chèvre
30ml lemon-infused olive oil

Slice each artichoke in half lengthways and set aside. If using, finely slice the lemon into 12 paper-thin slices. Cut each walnut into three, reserving two whole walnuts.

Toss together in a bowl the rocket, sliced walnuts, olive oil and balsamic. Lay out the ham slices perfectly flat on a clean board — they must not have any tears or holes. Using a palette knife, smear one-sixth of the chèvre over each piece of ham, then place half an artichoke on top with the stalk protruding beyond the edge, allowing enough room so that the ham slice can be rolled up to enclose the artichoke and rocket. Divide the rocket salad into six portions and lay over each artichoke half, allowing the leaves to protrude beyond both edges. If using preserved lemon, place a sliver at each end on top of the rocket. Roll up tightly and cut each length into three pieces, then arrange them on six plates. The middle piece should sit flat while the two end pieces should sit on their cut end with part of the artichoke stalk uppermost from one and rocket from the other. Keep at room temperature until ready to serve. Just before serving, shave the last two walnut pieces over each plate (use a truffle slicer or grater), then drizzle with lemon-infused oil.

Note: If the preserved lemon is used, it is quite salty and in combination with the ham no further seasoning will be required. Even without the lemon, exercise caution when seasoning.

SIMON SAYS *Serve a bottle of Malpighi aged balsamic vinegar for your guests to drizzle over the dish to add a smart touch.*

SERVES 6

ROCKET & MANCHEGO SALAD WITH TOASTED PINE NUTS, PEAR & DATES

This salad has featured very successfully on our Euro menu for some time and will continue to feature, particularly in the summer months. The pear and Manchego cheese are a delightful duo and the nuts and dates add a dimension that is very pleasing in a salad. I use the very special Prelibato aged white balsamic vinegar because of its sweetness. Aged traditional balsamic is a noble substitute but it must be of very good quality and most definitely aged. We are talking genuine balsamic here, not the vile vinegar that gets no closer to the real balsamic than the name on the label.

3 tbsp pine nuts
60g Manchego cheese
120g pears, *table ripe*
120g rocket *(arugula)*
12 dates, *pitted and roughly chopped*
Murray River salt or good quality flake salt
2 tbsp olive oil
1 tbsp Prelibato white balsamic vinegar

salad

In a sauté pan, toast the pine nuts over a medium–low heat until golden in colour, then transfer to a cold oven tray to stop them colouring any further. Using a vegetable peeler, shave the Manchego into paper-thin slivers.

Thinly slice the pears and place in a bowl with the rocket, dates, cheese and pine nuts. Season with salt, then pour over the olive oil and balsamic vinegar. Toss the salad and divide between six individual bowls or present in one large bowl. Serve immediately.

SERVES 6

STEAK TARTARE WITH WHITE TRUFFLE OIL & PARMIGIANO-REGGIANO

Legend tells us that the Tatar people of Central Asia did not have time to cook. They would place their meat underneath their horse's saddle and after a day's riding, the heat generated would have cooked the meat to some extent. I guess one could regulate the degree of tenderness by selecting an appropriate weight for the rider or perhaps riding until later in the day — an early variation of the weight-for-age calculation. Whatever the technique, it all seems a bit tedious to me. I strongly suggest you follow the instructions below rather than risking the ire of the SPCA or maybe even incurring a road tax.

Many people baulk at even the suggestion of consuming raw meat, but the reality is that the brandy, lemon juice, Tabasco sauce, salt, mustard and Worcestershire sauce all contribute towards marinating the meat, which I would argue is the same as cooking it. Whatever the pros and cons, you can't argue either way until you have tried it.

600g eye fillet steak
5 tbsp finely chopped pickled gherkins
5 tbsp finely chopped capers
4 tbsp finely chopped parsley
6 tbsp finely diced red onion
2 tbsp brandy
3 tbsp Worcestershire sauce
2 tsp Tabasco chipotle pepper sauce
  (smoked)
1 tbsp tomato paste
1 tbsp tomato ketchup
1 tbsp Dijon mustard
8 egg yolks
1 tsp lemon juice
1 tsp salt
½ tsp ground black pepper

tartare

In a food processor, chop the steak very finely but do not reduce it to a paste. Transfer it to a mixing bowl and set aside. Mix 4 tablespoons of chopped gherkin, 3½ tablespoons of chopped capers, 2 tablespoons of chopped parsley and 4 tablespoons of chopped red onion into the chopped steak, reserving the balance in separate containers to use as garnish. Add the brandy, Worcestershire and Tabasco sauces, tomato paste, tomato ketchup and mustard and combine well with a fork. Mix in two of the egg yolks until they are well combined, then gently mix in the lemon juice, salt and pepper until the mixture is glossy and holds together nicely.

1 medium loaf ciabatta
2 tbsp olive oil

ciabatta

Preheat the oven grill. Slice the ciabatta into 1cm thick slices. Brush each slice liberally with olive oil, then toast both sides under the medium–high oven grill until golden and crisp.

1 tbsp white truffle oil
100g Parmigiano-Reggiano

assembly

Divide the tartare mixture into six portions and gently roll each into a ball, taking care not to overmix. Transfer the balls to individual plates, then make a small indentation in the middle of each (the best way of doing this is to use an egg as a tool, pressing the wide end into the tartare to make the indentation). Place an egg yolk into each indentation, then garnish with cracked pepper. Stack some toasted ciabatta onto each plate and drizzle with the truffle oil. Use the leftover parsley, onion, capers and gherkin to garnish the plate. Finally, shave the cheese into curls using a potato peeler and place some around each plate.

SERVES 6

SCALLOPS ON BALSAMIC ONIONS & CRAB MASHED POTATO WITH CHAMPAGNE & GREEN PEA HOLLANDAISE

Scallops get my vote as the best shellfish. Unique for more than just their decorative and distinctive shell, they are active swimmers, so you can advertise them on your menu as 'free-range scallops'. They are, in fact, the only migratory bivalves. They can and do change sex, with both male and female producing roe; red if the current sex is female, and white if male. It's my guess that when one encounters some mottled red and white roe, the unfortunate scallop must have suffered some sort of gender identity crisis, but even these ones take a lot of beating as a culinary treat.

green pea purée

500ml water
1 tbsp salt
1 tsp sugar
90g green peas, *fresh or frozen*

Bring the water, salt and sugar to the boil, then add the peas and cook for 3–4 minutes until they are very soft. Strain the peas, retaining 3 tablespoons of the cooking liquid and 2 tablespoons of peas. Transfer the hot peas and the reserved liquid to a food processor and blend until smooth, then pass the purée through a sieve. Set aside until ready to use.

hollandaise

60ml Champagne or white wine
150g butter, *unsalted*
3 egg yolks
90g green pea purée
1½ tsp flake salt
¼ tsp white pepper

In a small saucepan, bring the Champagne or wine to the boil and reduce by half, then set aside. Melt the butter in a medium-sized saucepan over a low heat. Once the butter has melted, remove the pan from the heat. Using a spoon, skim off the foam from the surface of the melted butter and discard. Transfer the rest of the butter to a warmed pouring jug and set aside.

In a 20cm diameter stainless steel bowl, combine the egg yolks and reduced wine and whisk until frothy. Place the bowl over an 18cm saucepan of simmering but not boiling water and continue to whisk the egg yolks for 2–3 minutes or until they begin to thicken. Remove the bowl from the heat and continue to whisk the eggs for a further 1 minute to allow the eggs to cool down (doing this on a cold bench will assist the cooling process). Place the bowl containing the whisked eggs back into the saucepan, but remove it from the heat. Very slowly pour the melted butter, leaving the milk solids behind, into the egg yolk mixture, whisking continuously as you do so. Whisk in the pea purée and blend thoroughly. Season with salt and white pepper.

SIMON SAYS *When making hollandaise sauce, the correct water temperature is of paramount importance. It should simmer, not boil, and the base of the container should not be in contact with the simmering water. If there is too much heat, the eggs will scramble and overcook. On the other hand, if the water is not hot enough, the sauce may separate. It is a slow and steady process that cannot be rushed.*

The microwave is a useful tool to produce the required clarified butter, but take care to have the container covered to avoid butter explosions. Use a very low heat.

Take particular care when adding the butter to the sauce; it must be done a little at a time, while you are continuously whisking. If too much

butter is added at once, the sauce may not thicken. Egg yolks can only cope with absorbing a certain amount of butter, so if too much butter is incorporated the sauce will inevitably curdle.

If the sauce starts to separate, add 1–2 tablespoons of cream and beat the sauce with a wire whisk until it is smooth again. If the sauce curdles, you can put it in a blender and process it, but this will alter the texture so is really a last-resort measure.

assembly

Remove the crab meat from the shells. Heat the mashed potato and add the cipolline onions and crab meat and keep hot. Ensure the scallops are thoroughly dry before cooking — wet scallops will simply boil or steam. Just prior to cooking, season the scallops with salt and pepper. Heat the olive oil in a sauté pan to a shimmer, then add the butter and the seasoned scallops. Sauté the scallops until they have just firmed up and are hot in the middle (about 30 seconds). Take care not to overcook them or they will become tough and rubbery.

Divide the hot potato mix evenly between the plates, then place a portion of scallops to the side of the mash. Using a serving spoon, drizzle over the pea hollandaise and garnish with the reserved green peas, cut in half.

SERVES 6

300g Alaskan red king crab legs
600g mashed potato *(see page 232)*
90g chopped cipolline onions in balsamic
600g scallops
salt and pepper
40ml olive oil
25g butter

DUET OF DUCK BREAST & IBÉRICO BELLOTA HAM WITH MUSCAT DRESSING & FOIE GRAS & GREEN PEPPERCORN ICE CREAM

Ibérico ham is the latest obsession of the food world and is giving Italian prosciutto more than a run for its money. The very best is aged for up to two years and is in the same league as osciètre caviar as far as price is concerned. The black pigs that are the source of Ibérico ham are raised free-range in Spain's oak forests and are fattened on a diet of grain and acorns. The most prized pigs, sold as jamón ibérico de bellota, roam free for their entire lives, foraging for acorns. Enthusiasts claim that the fat is as healthy as virgin olive oil, but this is stretching things a bit. What can be claimed, however, is that you will never taste a better ham or a fat as good as this.

½ tbsp yellow mustard seeds
3 tbsp water
60g brown sugar
100ml muscat wine
60g chilli grape jam *(see page 231)*
¼ tsp salt
100ml Pukara extra-virgin olive oil

dressing

It's best to complete the dressing a day in advance to allow the mustard seeds to soften. Soak the mustard seeds in 1 tablespoon of water. Combine the remaining 2 tablespoons of water with the brown sugar in a small saucepan. Place the sugar and water over a medium heat, stirring with a wooden spoon for 3 minutes until the sugar has lightly caramelised. Add the muscat, bring to the boil and simmer for 3 minutes, until the sugar has dissolved. Pour into a blender and add the chilli grape jam. Blend until a smooth texture is achieved, then pour into a bowl. Add the drained mustard seeds and salt and whisk together, simultaneously drizzling in the olive oil very slowly until all the oil has been added and a nice, glossy, thick sauce is achieved.

15 green peppercorns
500ml trim milk
4 egg yolks
120g caster sugar
100g can foie gras

ice cream

Crush or finely chop the peppercorns. Heat the milk and peppercorns until the mixture reaches a simmer, then remove from the heat and set aside. Blend the egg yolks and caster sugar together in a food processor until creamed. Transfer to a bain-marie. Gradually pour the warm milk into the egg and sugar mixture, stirring to combine. Keep stirring until the mixture coats the back of a spoon or reaches 83°C on a sugar thermometer. Cool the bowl over ice, still stirring. If you have a Pacojet transfer the mixture to a Pacojet beaker along with the foie gras and freeze; pacotise prior to assembly. Alternatively transfer the cooled mixture to a blender, add the foie gras and blend until combined. Refrigerate for 30 minutes. Once chilled, transfer to an ice cream machine and churn following the manufacturer's instructions.

42g Parmigiano-Reggiano, *grated*

parmigiano baskets

Divide the grated cheese into six portions. Spread them, one at a time, in the shape of a 4.5cm diameter circle on a small plate. Microwave for 45 seconds or until the cheese melts. Wait for 10 seconds then, using a palette knife, lift the melted cheese and lay it over the top of a wine cork or wine bottle top, allowing the sides to hang down. Leave to cool for a few minutes, during which time it will go crispy. Repeat the process to make seven parmigiano baskets (one spare, as they are fragile). Store the baskets in an airtight container until required.

3 duck breasts
salt and pepper
1 tbsp olive oil

duck breast

Place the duck breasts skin-side down on a chopping board and trim off any excess fat and sinew. Turn each one over and, with the tip of a very sharp knife, score the top of the fat lightly to make a criss-cross pattern. Season with salt and pepper. Pour the olive oil into a frying pan and heat to a shimmer. One at a time, place the duck breasts in the pan, skin-side down. Sauté over a medium heat for 7 minutes then turn the breast over and sear the other side for 3 minutes. Remove from the pan and rest for 8 minutes on a plate lined with paper towels.

6 slices Ibérico Bellota Gran Reserva

special equipment *Pacojet or ice cream machine*

assembly

Slice each duck breast into 10 even slices. Arrange one slice of ham, five slices of duck breast and a Parmigiano basket on each plate. Drizzle with the muscat dressing and place a scoop of ice cream into each basket. Serve immediately.

SERVES 6

CRISPY TEMPURA OYSTERS ON AN ONION PURÉE WITH SMOKED SALMON YOGHURT

The smoked salmon yoghurt sphere in this recipe utilises the exciting El Bulli Texturas Algin and Calcic products. What one is able to achieve with these fascinating culinary aids is nothing short of phenomenal, and to date I believe we have barely scratched the surface of the textures and decorative effects. If you wish to adopt a more straightforward approach, go with option two: a smoked salmon yoghurt dip served in the oyster shell.

100g cipolline onions
1 cup milk

onion purée

In a small saucepan, cover the onions with the milk and bring to the boil. Simmer for 25 minutes, stirring so the milk doesn't catch on the bottom. Strain the onions through a sieve, discarding the milk. Purée the onions in a high-speed blender until smooth, then pour into a plastic squeeze bottle with a fine nozzle. Keep warm until ready to use.

125g hot-smoked salmon
250g yoghurt
1 tsp chipotle Tabasco chipotle pepper sauce (smoked)
2g Texturas Calcic
1 tbsp wasabi tobiko caviar
15g spring onion, finely chopped
salt and pepper
1 litre mineral water
3.2g Texturas Algin

salmon sphere (option one)

Place the smoked salmon into a food processor and blend until it forms a paste. Add the yoghurt and Tabasco sauce and combine. Add the Calcic and blend for a further 10 seconds. Pour into a container and fold in the wasabi tobiko caviar and spring onion. Season with salt and pepper and set aside until ready to use.

Pour half of the mineral water into a clean high-speed blender, along with the Algin. Blend for 5 seconds, transfer to a bowl and set aside. This will be referred to later in the recipe as the Algin water bath.

125g hot-smoked salmon
250g yoghurt
1 tsp chipotle Tabasco chipotle pepper sauce (smoked)
1 tbsp wasabi tobiko caviar
15g spring onion, finely chopped

salmon dip (option two)

In a blender, combine the smoked salmon, yoghurt and Tabasco sauce and blend to form a purée. Pour into a container and fold in the wasabi tobiko caviar and spring onion. Divide the mixture between six oyster shells.

166gm Trisol (optional)
1100ml soda water
333g tempura flour

tempura batter

Mix together the Trisol and the soda water. Pour over the tempura flour and whisk until combined. Alternatively, omit the Trisol and increase the amount of flour to 500g, then whisk together with the soda water.

1 litre canola oil
3 dozen oysters
½ cup plain flour
salt

oysters

Heat the canola oil in a large saucepan to 180°C (test with a thermometer, as the temperature is important). Once the oil has reached the correct temperature, roll the oysters through plain flour, dip them into the tempura batter and drop them — three at a time — into the heated oil until the batter becomes crisp. As the oysters are cooked, remove them from the oil and gently roll them on a paper towel to drain excess oil. A sharp-pointed knife is useful to check the internal temperature of the oysters until an appropriate cooking time is established. Ensure the temperature of the oil has returned to 180°C before cooking the next batch. Season with salt.

6 chives, *cut in half*
1 lemon, *cut into wedges*

special equipment *basic spherification kit, Texturas tool kit*

assembly

If making the salmon spheres, pour the remaining 500ml of mineral water into a small bowl. Fill the Texturas tablespoon measure with the smoked salmon mix, then carefully pour it into the Algin water bath, leaving it to semi-solidify for 2 minutes. Using the Texturas slotted spoon, remove the sphere from the bath and rinse it in the remaining mineral water. As you complete each sphere (one for each diner), place it in an empty oyster shell. Place a shell containing a sphere on each plate. Squeeze three small blobs of onion purée on to each plate, then arrange some battered oysters in the middle and garnish with 2 chive halves and a lemon wedge. If not making spheres, place an oyster shell containing smoked salmon purée on each plate and then arrange as above.

SIMON SAYS *The Trisol makes the batter very crispy and does not absorb nearly as much oil as flour does during the cooking.*

SERVES 6

JERVOIS STEAK HOUSE

AND SALOON
The Steak House to end all arguments

accommodated with pleasure. Good eating

Desserts

Chocolate pudding
a sambuca balsamic chocolate ice cream

Fruit pie
a mint chocolate & vanilla ice cream

Summer salads
english cream, a strawberry & balsamic

NATURAL BLUFF OYSTERS WITH CUCUMBER MARTINI SORBET

Some say that Bluff oysters, grown slowly in the cold clean waters of Foveaux Strait, are the finest in the world and I have no argument with this view. In season, they are dredged by Bluff's oyster fleet. In 1970, with 23 boats operating, the permitted catch quota amounted to the consumption of two dozen oysters by every man, woman and child in the country. No commerical oyster catches were permitted during the seasons of 1991–1994 because of the Bonamia parasite. Oyster harvesting was resumed with a limited number of boats and small quotas. Given our appetite for oysters there must have been some serious withdrawal symptoms apparent during the closed seasons!

840ml water
30 cucumber slices, *1mm thick*

frozen shot glasses
Into each of the six plastic containers pour 140ml of water, then add 5 slices of cucumber. Place a shot glass in the middle of each, position on a flat tray and freeze for 24 hours.

45ml gin
1 tbsp vermouth
240g telegraph cucumber, *peeled, chopped and deseeded*
50ml sugar syrup *(see page 232)*
2 small mint leaves
1 tbsp fresh lime juice

cucumber martini sorbet
Place the gin, vermouth, cucumber, sugar syrup, mint leaves and lime juice in a blender and blend until the mixture is smooth and the cucumber totally combined. Pour into an ice cream churn and follow the manufacturer's instructions. Alternatively, pour into a container and freeze until solid. When frozen, remove from the container, break into pieces small enough to fit into the food processor and process until of 'smoothie' consistency, then return to the freezer.

If using a Pacojet, place all ingredients into the pacojet canister and freeze for 24 hours. Once frozen, pacotise the entire canister, then refreeze and pacotise again.

3 dozen Bluff *or your favourite oysters in the half shell*

assembly
Turn the frozen bases out of the containers — use a little running warm water to help you do this. Place each one on a plate with nine oysters in their half shells in a circle around it. Pour any oyster juice over them. Use a tablespoon to scrape the sorbet into shavings. Spoon the sorbet into the shot glasses and serve immediately.

special equipment 6 x 60ml ice-cold shot glasses, 6 x 7.5cm round x 5cm deep plastic containers (the ones that Bluff oysters are sold in are perfect), ice cream machine or Pacojet (optional)

SIMON SAYS *If you have some Prelibato white balsamic vinegar, a couple of drops on each oyster is a great alternative to the oyster juice.*

SERVES 4

BLUFF OYSTERS WITH PRELIBATO WITH A LIME & CRACKED BLACK PEPPER SORBET

Nelson or Cloudy Bay oysters are a suitable substitute for Bluff oysters. I swear by Prelibato white balsamic vinegar, produced by the Acetaia Malpighi company in Italy, a fifth-generation family balsamic producer which, in addition to producing some of the finest traditional balsamics, has also developed this wonderful white balsamic. What makes Prelibato so special is that it's made from the must of white grapes and aged in ash barrels for six years. The resulting taste is quite remarkable: sweet, full-bodied and incredibly full-flavoured.

500ml water
150g caster sugar
1 tbsp liquid glucose
100ml lime juice
4 black peppercorns, *freshly ground*

3 cups ice cubes
2 spring onions, *finely sliced*

18 Bluff oysters or oysters of choice
50ml Prelibato white balsamic vinegar

special equipment *ice cream machine or Pacojet (optional), 6 x 25cm round x 5cm deep terrine moulds, melon baller*

sorbet
Pour the water into a heavy-bottomed saucepan and add the caster sugar, glucose and lime juice. Place over a medium heat and simmer for 10 minutes. Remove from the heat and add the peppercorns. Pour into a Pacojet cannister or ice cream machine and follow the manufacturer's instructions. Alternatively, pour into a container and freeze until solid. When frozen, remove from the container, break into pieces small enough to fit into the food processor and process until of 'smoothie' consistency, then return to the freezer.

garnish
Freeze 6 x 20cm x 5cm terrine moulds, each filled with 2cm of water and topped up with a jumble of ice cubes and spring onions.

assembly
Remove the terrine-shaped ice from each of the frozen terrine moulds — use a little running warm water to help you do this. Place each one on a plate and top with three oysters in their shells. Drizzle each oyster with some Prelibato white balsamic vinegar. To finish, use a melon baller to make a ball of sorbet to place on each oyster.

SERVES 6

soup

SWEET WILD ONION & CAULIFLOWER SOUP

Cauliflower doesn't need any explantion, but cipolline onions (pronounced chip-oh-LEE-nay), available in cans and jars, usually preserved in balsamic vinegar, are a bit less familiar and somewhat more difficult to find. However some of the better supermarkets and of course delicatessans stock them. Their flesh is a yellowish color and their skin is thin and papery, ranging in colour from pale yellow to the light brown of Spanish onions. Cipolline are sweeter, with more residual sugar than the garden-variety white or yellow onions, but not as much as shallots. An advantage of using cipolline onions is that they are small and flat, making them ideal for roasting. This, combined with their sweetness, makes them a lovely addition to recipes where you might want to use whole caramelised onions.

200g cauliflower
1 tbsp Pukara extra-virgin olive oil
60g white-skinned onion, *sliced*
10g garlic, *crushed*
400ml vegetable stock
20g butter
90ml cream
salt
white pepper

100g cipolline onions in balsamic
²/₃ cup milk

special equipment *6 demitasse cups, medium-sized plastic squeeze bottle*

cauliflower soup

Cut the cauliflower into small pieces and set aside. Heat the olive oil until it starts to shimmer. Add the onion and garlic and cook for 3 minutes without colouring. Add the cauliflower, stock, butter and cream. Bring to a simmer and cook for 15 minutes. Once cooked, purée in a high-speed blender until smooth and creamy. Season with salt and pepper then pour into a clean saucepan and set aside until needed.

onion purée

Cover the cipolline onions with the milk in a medium-sized saucepan and bring to the boil. Simmer for 25 minutes, stirring continuously, so the milk doesn't catch on the bottom. Once cooked, strain the onions through a sieve and then discard the milk. Purée the onions in a high-speed blender until smooth. Pour into a medium-sized plastic squeeze bottle with a fine nozzle. Keep warm ready for use.

assembly

Reheat the cauliflower soup, then pour into a serving jug. Pour equal portions of the soup into the demitasse cups, then swirl some onion purée from the squeeze bottle over the top of each cup.

SIMON SAYS *When you cook the onions, the balsamic vinegar will cause the milk to split; this is normal.*

This soup is a great light entrée. If you happen to have some truffle oil in your pantry, a couple of drops on top is a sensational addition.

SERVES 6

DUET OF ROSEMARY BUTTERNUT & PEPPERED POTATO SOUP TOPPED WITH TRUFFLE CREAM

Each of these soups can be served separately and is pretty impressive in its own right. If serving the butternut soup alone, replace the rosemary with the grated zest of half an orange or add a little curry powder while sautéing the onion, leek and garlic; I would also recommend blending some sautéed peeled apple into the soup along with the pumpkin. From a presentation point of view, I prefer to serve the two together as described below. The truffle cream also makes a great dip with raw celery or crusty bread.

500g butternut pumpkin
3 tbsp Pukara extra-virgin olive oil
1 small white-skinned onion, *roughly chopped*
1 leek, white stalk only, *roughly chopped*
2 medium cloves garlic, *roughly chopped*
1 tbsp honey
850ml vegetable stock
1 sprig rosemary, *very finely chopped*
100ml cream
20g butter
salt and pepper

25g butter
500g potatoes, *peeled and roughly chopped (Agria if available)*
1 small onion, *roughly chopped*
2 medium cloves garlic, *roughly chopped*
½ tbsp ground black peppercorns
½ tsp salt
1 litre vegetable stock
150ml cream

150g mascarpone
½ tsp black truffle cream
¼ tsp truffle oil
1 spring onion, *roughly chopped*
salt and pepper
4 slices truffle or 1 tbsp chopped chives

rosemary butternut soup

Preheat the oven to 180°C. Cut each butternut in half and remove the seeds. Roast until tender (about 45 minutes), then leave to cool. Scrape the cooled flesh from the skin.

In a saucepan, heat the olive oil to a shimmer. Add the onion, leek and garlic and cook over a medium heat until the onion is translucent. Add the butternut flesh, honey and stock. Bring to the boil. Reduce the heat, add the rosemary and simmer for 10 minutes. Transfer to a blender and purée, then pour into a clean saucepan and stir through the cream and butter. Season to taste with salt, pepper and additional honey if desired. If the soup is too thick, add more stock and/or cream.

peppered potato soup

Melt the butter in a saucepan over a medium heat. Add the potato, onion, garlic, black pepper and salt and sauté until the onion is translucent. Add the stock, bring to the boil and simmer for 25 minutes or until the potato is soft. Add the cream, then purée the soup in a blender or food processor. Taste and adjust the seasoning. If the soup is too thick, add more stock and/or cream.

truffle cream

In a mixing bowl, combine the mascarpone, black truffle cream, truffle oil, spring onion, salt and pepper. As mentioned in the recipe introduction, this truffle cream also has a solo role as a dip if desired, and is particularly good with raw vegetables, such as celery or carrot or, if you must, potato crisps.

assembly

In separate saucepans, bring both soups back to the boil. Once hot, transfer each to its own pouring jug, then pour both soups simultaneously into separate sides of the serving bowl, so they flow toward one another, but do not combine. Float a teaspoon of truffle cream on top of the soup. If budget permits, add a slice of truffle or alternatively top with some chopped chives.

SERVES 4

GREEN PEA SOUP WITH POACHED QUAIL EGG, PANCETTA CHIPS & TRUFFLE OIL

Chefs don't often get invited to people's homes for dinner; there seems to be a fear that when served a beautiful home-cooked meal, we will suddenly grow horns and become food critics! My idea of a meal to die for is a roast and veg, preferably with some sweet frozen baby peas as an accompaniment. Two of my all-time favourite customers, Kevin and Rowena Roberts, insist that I serve this green pea soup for them on a regular basis. The pancetta in it is belly pork, which has been salt cured for about three months; it can be flavoured with all manner of herbs including nutmeg, fennel, peppers and sometimes garlic.

2½ tbsp Pukara extra-virgin olive oil
½ medium onion
2 medium cloves garlic
650g frozen peas, *not minted*
850ml vegetable stock
½ cup cream
salt and white pepper

pea soup
In a large saucepan, heat the olive oil to a shimmer. Add the onion and garlic and cook over a medium heat until they become soft and transparent. Add the peas, then pour in the vegetable stock. Bring to the boil and simmer for 10 minutes. Rapidly cool the contents in an ice bath (this ensures the peas retain their great colour). When cold, purée in a high-speed blender until smooth, then pass through a sieve. Add the cream, season with salt and pepper to taste and keep chilled until ready to reheat.

1 litre water
100ml white wine vinegar
6 quail eggs
bowl of iced water

poached quail eggs
In a medium-sized saucepan, bring the water and vinegar to the boil. Reduce the heat so that the water is just simmering. Crack the quail eggs and place the contents of each one into a separate ramekin. Holding the ramekin just above the surface of the water, carefully slide the egg into the simmering water. Poach for 45 seconds, then remove from the water with a slotted spoon and place into the bowl of iced water.

8 slices pancetta, *1mm thick x 15cm long*

pancetta chips
Preheat the grill to medium-high. Place the pancetta on a wire oven rack under the preheated grill and cook until golden and crispy (about 4 minutes). Remove and place on paper towels to absorb the excess fat.

1 tbsp white truffle oil

assembly
Place approximately 1 litre of water in a small saucepan over a high heat and bring to the boil. Remove from the heat. Heat the pea soup in a separate saucepan. Warm four serving bowls. Place the quail eggs into the saucepan containing the hot water and leave to warm through for up to 30 seconds. Ladle the soup evenly into the warm bowls, remove the eggs from the hot water using a slotted spoon and place one in the middle of each soup bowl. Place two pieces of pancetta on top, lightly drizzle with the truffle oil and serve.

SERVES 4

FRENCH ONION SOUP SERVED IN A COB LOAF

One of the first jobs any rookie or apprentice chef gets is peeling onions. There may not be any onions required for the daily prep, but you still get to peel them. The ability to get through this task without shedding buckets of tears is guaranteed to infuriate a sadistic head chef and if you can manage this, it makes your day. My early apprentice days with the legendary Tony Astle were no exception. I tried every way known to man to stay on top, including taking my own carefully pre-chilled onions. Trust me, none of the clever schemes worked. I found the only way to get through was to pray that the restaurant would prosper so that someone more junior would eventually be employed to take over onion-peeling duties.

Legend has it that onion soup was created by King Louis XV of France. Late one night, he discovered he had only onions, butter and champagne at his hunting lodge, so he mixed them together to create the first French onion soup. I'm sceptical — I believe a more likely scenario is that the champagne was consumed by King Louis and his entourage while some poor snivelling kid peeled the onions so the royals could have them fried in butter.

onion soup

1.5kg brown onions
4 bay leaves
1 tsp black peppercorns
1200ml dry riesling
2 litres beef stock
3 tbsp vegetable stock powder
¼ tsp white pepper
salt

Finely slice the onions and place in a large, heavy-based saucepan. Place over a medium–low heat, add the bay leaves and peppercorns, then sauté the onions until they start to caramelise and turn a dark amber colour. This will take about 1 hour. Add the wine, beef stock and vegetable stock powder. Reduce until a soup consistency is achieved (approximately another hour). Season with pepper and salt to taste.

SIMON SAYS *Caramelising onions involves cooking onions very slowly until the sugar in the onions melts and very nearly burns, turning brown in the process. While caramelisation can be achieved within 30 minutes, I prefer to allow at least 1 full hour of cooking to bring out the complex flavours.*

cob loaves

6 tbsp butter
2 medium cloves garlic, minced
6 x 500g cob-style sourdough loaves

Mix the butter and garlic together and set aside. Cut a 2cm slice off the top of each loaf to form a lid. Using a spoon, hollow out the centre of each loaf to form a 'soup bowl' (taking care not to puncture the walls). Brush the inside of the loaves with the garlic butter.

assembly

60ml cognac
200g Gruyère cheese, *grated*
1 tbsp chopped parsley

Preheat the oven to 180°C. Reheat the soup, adding the cognac. Place the hollowed-out cob loaves and their lids in the oven for a few minutes until they are lightly toasted and become crisp. Place the toasted cob loaves in warm bowls and fill with the soup. Top with Gruyère cheese, then carefully place the soup-filled loaves under the grill until the cheese begins to melt and turn golden-brown. Sprinkle with chopped parsley. Serve with the bread lids on the side.

SERVES 6

SHED 5 SEAFOOD CHOWDER SERVED IN A COB LOAF WITH FRESH FISH, SCALLOPS, PRAWNS & GREEN-LIPPED MUSSELS

This is a novel way of serving chowder and is sensationally popular with diners at our Shed 5 restaurant. The preparation is somewhat involved but the results are worth every second of the time spent in preparing the dish.

3 x 400g cans Italian whole peeled
    tomatoes
200g tomato paste
2kg crayfish bodies
100g butter
50ml oil
2 onions, *roughly diced*
1 carrot, *roughly diced*
2 stalks celery, *roughly diced*
100ml brandy
200ml white wine
2 litres fish stock

crayfish bisque

Preheat the oven to 180°C. Drain the tomatoes, reserving the juice. Place tomatoes on a baking tray and roast for 90 minutes (this will deepen the colour and enrich the flavour of the tomatoes).

In a small saucepan, cook the tomato paste for 3 minutes over a medium heat, stirring constantly so it doesn't catch (cooking the paste removes any bitterness from the paste and also deepens the colour). Remove from the heat and set aside. Place the crayfish bodies in a heavy saucepan. Using a large wooden spoon, crush the bodies into pieces as small as possible. Alternatively, crush them using a butcher's knife on a chopping board. Transfer the pieces to a food processor and pulse them to create a crunchy, paste-like mixture (this will allow maximum flavour extraction).

In another saucepan, melt the butter and oil together, then cook the crayfish paste for 8 minutes. Add the chopped vegetables and continue to cook for a further 5 minutes, then add the cooked tomato paste. Pour in the brandy and white wine and allow the mixture to reduce by half over the heat. Stir in the roasted tomatoes, reserved tomato juice and fish stock and bring to the boil. Simmer for 30 minutes. Pass the bisque through a fine mouli to extract as much liquid as possible, then pass through a sieve to remove any remaining shell or large matter. You should now have approximately 1.2 litres of bisque; if you have more, return it to the heat and reduce until the correct quantity is reached.

150g butter
150g flour
1.3 litres fish stock
1.2 litres crayfish bisque *(see above)*
salt
ground black pepper

chowder base

In a medium-sized saucepan, melt the butter, add the flour and cook for 5 minutes, stirring continuously to avoid the mixture sticking or browning. Add the fish stock, very little at first and very gradually, so that the resulting paste is progressively thinned. It is better to incorporate the stock off the heat to avoid lumps. Add no more than one cup at a time, stirring continuously until the liquid has been completely absorbed before adding the next cup. Repeat until all the fish stock has been added. (If the stock has been added off the heat, return the pan to the hob and cook until thickened.) Pass through a sieve to remove any lumps. Return the base to the saucepan and add the crayfish bisque. Gently bring to the boil, and adjust the seasoning if desired (don't add too much salt because cooked shellfish, which are salty in themselves, will be added later).

60g butter

2 medium cloves garlic, *minced*

6 x 500g cob-style sourdough loaves

300ml cream *(optional)*

4 tbsp Pernod

24 prawn tails, *shelled*

60ml white wine

6 green-lipped mussels, *steamed*

180g fresh white fish, *cut into 2cm cubes*

12 fresh scallops

2 tbsp chopped chives

assembly

Heat the white wine in a saucepan with a lid. Add the mussels and cook with the lid on until they open. Discard any that do not open. Remove from the wine and when they are cool remove the meat from the shells. Clean away any residual beard, the brown foot and tough muscles. Return the meat to the shells and set aside. Preheat the oven to 180°C. Mix the butter and garlic together and set aside. Cut a 2cm slice off the top of each loaf to form a lid. Using a spoon, hollow out the centre of each loaf to form a 'soup bowl' (taking care not to puncture the walls). Brush the inside of the loaves and the underside of the lids with the garlic butter. Place the cob loaf shells and lids into the oven to lightly toast and become crisp. Add the cream and Pernod to the chowder base and gently reheat until simmering. Add the prawns, simmer for 1 minute, then add the mussels, fish and scallops and simmer again until they are cooked (remove a piece of fish and a scallop and cut through to test — the fish should be flaky and the scallop just hot in the middle). Place the loaves on the serving plates, then carefully pour in the chowder, ensuring the seafood is evenly distributed. Serve the toasted, buttered lids as a large crouton to the side of each plate and sprinkle with the chopped chives.

SIMON SAYS *As soon as the scallops are hot in the middle they are cooked; further cooking will make them rubbery.*

SERVES 6

CHILLED SUMMER TOMATO SOUP WITH CRAB & APPLE SALSA TOPPED WITH GAZPACHO SORBET

Gazpacho is a cold Spanish soup, originating from an ancient Andalusian concoction based on a combination of stale bread, garlic, olive oil, salt and vinegar. The ingredients have been modified for this recipe, transforming it into a sorbet. The crab and apple salsa on which the sorbet is bedded and the sorbet alone make wonderful little appetisers in addition to making up this complete chilled soup presentation.

25 vine-ripened tomatoes
2½ tbsp tomato paste
100ml tomato ketchup
1 tbsp Pukara extra-virgin olive oil
550ml tomato juice
500ml canned Italian whole peeled
   tomatoes
8 large basil leaves
2 tsp Tabasco chipotle pepper sauce
   (smoked)
½ tsp flaked salt

10 vine-ripened tomatoes
80g red capsicum
100g telegraph cucumber
400g can Italian whole peeled tomatoes
75ml tomato ketchup
1 tbsp Pukara extra-virgin olive oil
200ml tomato juice
3 large basil leaves
40g caster sugar
20g glucose

2 vine-ripened tomatoes
30g caster sugar
1 Granny Smith apple, *peeled and finely diced*
4 large basil leaves
5g (about 18) small coriander leaves
300g picked Alaskan red king crab meat
1 tsp finely diced fresh red chilli, *seeds removed*
1 tbsp Pukara extra-virgin olive oil

6 small basil leaves to garnish

special equipment *ice cream machine or Pacojet, 7cm x 3cm pastry cutter, mouli*

soup
Remove the seeds from the vine tomatoes and roughly chop the flesh into a large bowl. Add the tomato paste, ketchup, olive oil, tomato juice, whole peeled tomatoes, basil, Tabasco and salt. Marinate overnight. The next day, place the mixture in a blender and process until smooth. Pass through a mouli to remove any small seeds and adjust seasoning if required. Set aside.

SIMON SAYS *We use canned tomatoes because they are fully ripened before they are harvested and canned.*

gazpacho sorbet
Remove the seeds from the vine tomatoes and place the flesh in a large bowl. Halve the capsicum lengthways, remove the seeds and roughly chop the flesh. Repeat with the cucumber and add both to the bowl. Add the whole peeled tomatoes, ketchup, olive oil, tomato juice, basil leaves and sugar. Marinate for 3 hours. Place in a blender and process until smooth, then pass through a mouli. Put the glucose and half a cup of the mixture into a small saucepan. Bring to the boil to dissolve the glucose, allow to cool, then combine with the remaining tomato mix. Pour into an ice cream machine and churn following the manufacturer's instructions or pour into a Pacojet canister, freeze and pacotise once frozen.

salsa
Skin, deseed and dice the tomatoes as described on page 233 (tomato concasse). Pour 100ml of water into a small saucepan and add the sugar. Bring to the boil, then add the diced apple and simmer for 30 seconds. Leave to cool in the liquid. Tear the basil and coriander leaves into pieces. In a medium-sized bowl mix together the crab, basil, coriander, chilli and diced tomato. Strain and discard the water from the apple and add to the salad along with the olive oil and gently mix to combine.

assembly
Divide the salsa into six portions. Place the pastry cutter into the centre of each serving bowl and spoon one portion of salsa into it, packing it down gently. Repeat to make six nicely shaped mounds or islands. Pour 180ml of the soup around each of the salsa islands, then top with a scoop of the sorbet. Garnish with a small basil leaf.

SERVES 6

bird

ROTISSERIE CHICKEN RUBBED IN SIMON GAULT'S HERB RUB, SLOWLY COOKED ON THE ROTISSERIE & SERVED ON MASH WITH PEANUT SLAW

When Euro restaurant first opened I wanted the rotisserie to be a feature. To achieve that we had to produce a menu item that was not only appealingly different, it had to have staying power. I spent many hours blending different herb combinations but always with a strong Mediterranean influence and subsequently incinerated more chickens than I care to remember. The herb blend that we settled on remains unchanged to this day and this chicken still features on the menu at Euro. The ingredients suggest using the real deal, the original Simon Gault Herb Rub, which is commercially available. The substitute rub in the Building Blocks section is very much simplified and will not give the results that can be expected with the original blend.

3 size 11 chickens, *free-range organic*
90g Simon Gault Herb Rub *(see page 238)*

chicken

Remove any excess fat from the neck and bottom cavity of the chickens, then remove the wing tips by chopping through the outermost joint with a sharp knife. Using your fingers, loosen the skin from around the breast and thighs, then massage some of the herb rub under the skin. Liberally season the cavities with the rub as well as the inside and outside of the chickens. Truss with cooking string, ensuring that the wings and legs are tucked in close to the body. Place on a rotisserie skewer and cook on a preheated rotisserie for 1 hour or until the chicken has reached an internal temperature of 65°C (test by inserting a thermometer into the centre of the thickest part of the thigh). Remove the chicken from the rotisserie and place in a warm place to rest for 10 minutes. (If cooking in a conventional oven, preheat it to 180°C, place the chicken breast side up on a wire rack in a baking tray and roast for 1¼–1½ hours or until the juices run clear when the thickest part of the thigh is pierced with a skewer.)

1 cup mayonnaise *(see page 232)*
1 medium clove garlic, *minced*
½ head green cabbage
¼ head red cabbage
¼ cup roasted salted peanuts
1 tbsp chopped parsley
2 tbsp Saporoso aged balsamic vinegar
salt
ground black pepper to taste

peanut slaw

Mix the mayonnaise with the minced garlic and set aside. Remove the dry or perished outer leaves of both cabbage halves and discard. Cut in half again, then thinly slice. Place in a large mixing bowl with the peanuts, parsley and balsamic vinegar. Add enough of the mayonnaise to coat the slaw and season with salt and pepper to taste. Mix well.

mashed potato *(see page 232)*
500ml Madeira jus *(see page 232)*

special equipment *meat thermometer*

assembly

Preheat the oven to 200°C. Place the cooked chickens on a chopping board and insert a large chef's knife into each bird and cut along the inside of the backbone all the way to the neck. Remove the backbone by chopping along either side. Place the resulting chicken halves on the board, skin-side up, and cut diagonally, separating the breast and thigh. Transfer the chicken pieces to a baking tray and reheat in the oven for 5 minutes. Heat the mash in a saucepan or in the microwave and spoon onto warmed plates. Stack a breast and chicken thigh on each serving of mash, placing the breast on top of the thigh. Arrange the slaw on the plate next to the mash. Bring the Madeira jus to the boil. Pass it through a fine sieve, then pour over and around the chicken and mash.

SERVES 6

LONG ISLAND DUCK, LONG ISLAND CITRUS SAUCE WITH GOLDEN RAISIN COUSCOUS & PINK PEPPERCORN BRIOCHE BUTTER

Frankly I would fear for my life if this dish was ever removed from the menu. One of the all-time favourites, it was named Long Island Duck because of the sauce, which has its origins in the Long Island iced tea cocktail, first served in the late 1970s at the Oak Beach Inn in Babylon, Long Island, New York. The Long Island Duck or the Big Duck is a building in the shape of a duck located in Long Island. It was originally built in 1931 by duck farmer Martin Maurer, who sold ducks and duck eggs there. In these circumstances we didn't have much choice with the naming of this dish.

duck

3 size 22 ducks

Preheat the oven to 160°C. Using a boning knife, remove the wishbone. Trim off excess fat. Season the entire skin of each bird with salt and pepper. Skewer the ducks onto the rotisserie rod and cook on a preheated BBQ rotisserie for 1 hour and 10 minutes. Remove the cooked ducks from the rotisserie and place in a 160°C oven for 40 minutes. Remove from the oven and set aside in a warm place for 20 minutes — this will firm the duck, allowing easy portioning. (If cooking in a conventional oven, preheat it to 160°C and cook the ducks for 2 hours and 5 minutes; allow the same amount of time to cool.) Place the whole ducks on a chopping board, breast-side up, then use a boning knife to cut down the middle from one end to the other. Cut the breast away from the carcass of the first duck, keeping the knife as close to the ribcage as possible to minimise wastage. When the breast has been removed, place it on a baking tray ready for reheating. Remove the legs from the carcass and add them to the baking tray. Repeat this procedure with the other two ducks, then set the tray aside until ready to reheat and assemble.

Long Island citrus sauce

1 cup sugar
20ml white rum
20ml tequila
20ml gin
20ml triple sec
1 litre orange juice, *sieved*
1 tbsp cornflour

Make a caramel by placing the sugar and 100ml of water into a saucepan. Bring to the boil, brushing the sides of the pan with a wet pastry brush a few times to prevent any sugar crystals forming and burning. Allow the mixture to simmer until it begins to turn the colour of caramel, i.e. walnut brown. Just before this stage is reached, add the rum, tequila, gin and triple sec and flame the mixture (be careful not to burn yourself while doing this). Pour in the orange juice, then bring back to a simmer for 15 minutes. Make a smooth, runny paste by combining the cornflour with 2 tablespoons of water and whisk it into the sauce. Bring the sauce back to the boil, then pass through a fine sieve. Set aside until required.

25ml Pukara extra-virgin olive oil

350g instant couscous

360ml chicken or vegetable stock

2 tsp Pukara extra-virgin olive oil

½ red capsicum, *deseeded and finely diced*

200g orange kumara, *peeled and finely diced*

2 tsp Pukara extra-virgin olive oil

½ cup raisins

2 tbsp pine nuts

1 tbsp chopped chives

1 tbsp butter

salt

cracked black pepper

6 tbsp unsalted butter

1½ tbsp whole pink peppercorns

100g brioche

salt

6 sprigs of chervil

couscous

In a medium-sized mixing bowl, pour the first measure of olive oil over the couscous and mix well. Heat the stock, bringing it to the boil, and pour over the couscous. Cover with a lid and set aside for 5 minutes. Put the second measure of olive oil in a sauté pan over a medium heat and add the diced capsicum. Sauté until soft, then transfer to a large mixing bowl. Next sauté the kumara for 8 minutes in the third measure of olive oil, then add it to the capsicum. Stir through the raisins. Toast the pine nuts on a flat oven tray in a moderate oven (180°C) until they turn a golden-brown colour. When cool add to the kumara and capsicum mixture. Separate the couscous by gently rubbing it with your fingertips to produce a fine grain mixture, taking care not to squash the grains. Add the couscous to the vegetables along with the chopped chives and butter. Stir to combine and season with salt and pepper to taste.

brioche butter

Soften the butter in a warm place, taking care not to melt it. Blend the peppercorns to a fine dust in a blender. In a food processor, process the brioche until it resembles fine breadcrumbs. Combine the brioche crumbs, peppercorns and butter in a mixing bowl, season and mix well. Using a hot spoon, divide the mix into six portions. Transfer onto baking paper and set aside in the refrigerator to firm up.

assembly

Preheat the oven to 180°C. Place the baking tray of portioned ducks in the oven for 10 minutes or until hot. Heat the couscous in a microwave or in the oven (on a small oven tray) for 5 minutes. Reheat the sauce. Place the couscous in the centre of each plate, arrange the duck on the couscous and sit a portion of butter on top. Pour hot sauce over the duck and garnish with a sprig of chervil.

SERVES 6

PORTUGESE HONEY CITRUS DUCK WITH OLIVE BREAD MASH

Various accompaniments complement duck very well and the Chinese have long since perfected their choices. While I enjoy the Thai and Chinese flavours, I still find myself returning to the well-established partnering of duck and citrus, particularly when using farmed ducks, which today are far less fatty yet still feature that strong flavour; I believe citrus balances this superbly. Add an Asian honey influence along with the earthiness of the olive bread mash and there is little left to test the imagination other than choosing which wine to serve.

duck legs

120ml extra-virgin olive oil
1 large carrot, *chopped*
½ large onion, *chopped*
1 stick celery, *chopped*
6 medium cloves garlic
1 tsp lemon zest
1 tsp lime zest
1 tsp orange zest
3 bay leaves
½ stick lemongrass
3 kaffir lime leaves
½ tsp dried basil
1 tbsp turmeric
½ tbsp paprika
2 litres orange juice
250ml manuka honey
600ml water
6 size 22 duck legs

Preheat the oven to 180°C. Heat half of the olive oil to a shimmer in a large heatproof casserole dish, then add the carrot, onion, celery and garlic and sauté until golden brown. Add the zests, herbs and spices and half of the remaining oil and cook for a further 2 minutes. Stir in the orange juice, honey and water and cook slowly until the sauce has reduced by half.

Heat the remaining olive oil in a large sauté pan and add the duck legs, skin-side down. Cook until golden, then turn and cook for a further 2 minutes. Add the legs to the casserole dish and place in the oven for 1–1½ hours or until the meat is almost falling off the bone. Carefully remove the legs from the casserole and place on an oven tray ready for reheating. Pour all the liquid from the casserole dish into a saucepan and reduce over a high heat until it reaches sauce consistency, skimming any excess fat from the top as it heats. Strain and discard the solids, setting aside the sauce for reheating.

olive bread mash

300ml milk
240g stale ciabatta, *roughly cut*
150ml Pukara extra-virgin olive oil
300g mashed potato *(see page 232)*

In a small saucepan, warm through two-thirds of the milk, then add the ciabatta and allow to soak for 2 minutes. Remove the soaked bread to a saucepan and set aside. Heat the olive oil and remaining milk in a separate saucepan until just about to boil. Remove from the heat and pour the mixture very slowly into the bread over a low heat, while stirring with a wooden spoon. Quickly heat the mashed potato and fold it into bread and milk mixture. Season with salt and pepper to taste.

assembly

6 lime wedges

Preheat the oven to 180°C. Place the duck legs in the oven to heat through. Divide the olive bread mash between the serving bowls and top each with a duck leg. Pour over the sauce and garnish with a wedge of lime.

SERVES 6

TUNISIAN CHICKEN WITH SPICY COUSCOUS, TOASTED CAPERS & TOMATO

While I was in Sicily I was intrigued by a local restaurant with a very strong Tunisian influence. I talked my way into what I thought would be a session observing in the kitchen, but was greeted by the chef who with one hand gave me an apron and with the other a paper napkin on which he had scribbled a list of things he wanted done. This was a bit more than I had bargained for, but it was a great experience and, among other things, I learnt how to make couscous.

960g chicken thigh meat
50ml Pukara extra-virgin olive oil
½ tsp unsmoked paprika

2 tbsp Pukara extra-virgin olive oil
260g onions, *finely diced*
1 tbsp peeled and grated fresh ginger
3 medium cloves garlic, *finely chopped*
¼ hot red chilli, *finely chopped*
½ tsp unsmoked paprika
180g dates, *pitted*
180g raisins
1½ tbsp cumin
1½ tbsp curry powder
1½ tbsp coriander powder
6 cinnamon sticks
1 tbsp tomato paste
1 litre chicken stock

4 tbsp extra-virgin olive oil
360g couscous
350 ml chicken or vegetable stock
½ medium Beauregard kumara
½ small carrot
½ large stick of celery
1 red capsicum
½ small red onion, *finely diced*
¼ tsp ground cinnamon
¼ tsp ground coriander
¼ tsp ground cumin
1 tbsp chopped fresh coriander
1 tbsp chopped parsley
salt and pepper

150ml canola oil
3 tbsp capers
1 large courgette
1 red capsicum
1 tbsp butter
50ml canola oil
1 cup tomato concasse *(see page 233)*
coriander leaves to garnish

chicken
Roughly dice the chicken into 2.5cm cubes and place in a large mixing bowl. Add the oil and paprika and mix to combine. Set aside.

sauce
In a saucepan, heat the olive oil, then add the onion, ginger and garlic and sauté for 4 minutes over a low–medium heat. Add the chilli, paprika, dates, raisins, cumin, curry powder, coriander powder, cinnamon, tomato paste and chicken stock and bring to a simmer for 15–25 minutes until it reduces to achieve a runny sauce consistency. Set aside.

couscous
In a medium-sized mixing bowl pour half the olive oil over the couscous and mix well. Bring the stock to the boil and pour over the couscous. Cover with a lid and set aside for 10 minutes. Peel and finely dice the kumara, carrot and celery. Remove the core and seeds from the capsicum and finely dice the flesh. In a sauté pan heat the remaining 2 tablespoons of olive oil over medium heat and sauté the kumara, carrot and celery for 4 minutes. Add the onion and capsicum to the pan and sauté for a further 3 minutes. Finally add the sautéed vegetables to the couscous with all the remaining spice ingredients. Using a fork, gently mix until thoroughly combined, then taste and correct the seasoning if necessary.

assembly
Heat the canola oil to 160°C. Dry the capers, add to the oil and fry until crispy. Remove and drain on a paper towel. Cut the ends off the courgette, cut in half lengthways, then into batons. Cut the capsicum in half, remove the core and seeds and slice the flesh into strips. Heat the butter in a saucepan. Add the courgette and capsicum and sauté for 5 minutes over a medium heat, then add them to the sauce. Heat the second measure of canola oil in a medium-sized sauté pan and add the paprika-coated chicken mixture. Cook for a few minutes until the meat is cooked through. Combine the chicken and the sauce in another saucepan and cook over a low heat until hot. Reheat the couscous in the microwave. Add the tomato concasse and stir through the couscous. Divide the couscous evenly between six plates, then top each portion with the chicken mixture. Garnish with coriander leaves and fried capers.

SERVES 6

NEW YORK STRIP STEAK WITH KASUNDI TOMATO JUS & ONION RINGS

Sirloin is considered not quite fancy enough by many chefs but, along with Scotch fillet, it is one of my favourite cuts. Either could be used for this recipe. When of good quality and age and properly cooked, both these cuts have good flavour and can be impressively tender and moist. When buying the beef, bear in mind that the quality of the steak is the criterion by which the meal will be judged. It is my view that supermarket meat should never be used in preference to the properly aged and expertly presented cuts offered by a dedicated butchery. There is a place for supermarket meat, as my pets will confirm; generally beef or lamb presented good-side up and wrapped in plastic with a large red 'special' sticker as the supermarket day of death approaches should find its way to your table only via a long and intimate honeymoon in a casserole.

The accompanying onion rings are always a hit, the secret being not just coating them with breadcrumbs, but firstly dipping them in a tempura batter to seal them for greater crispness.

4 medium onions, *cut into 1cm thick rings*
milk, *to cover onion rings*
200g Japanese breadcrumbs
1 cup flour
tempura batter *(see page 233)*

3 tbsp Pukara extra-virgin olive oil
12g fenugreek seeds
12g black mustard seeds
12g cumin seeds
½ tsp turmeric powder
1 tsp curry powder
4 cloves garlic, *finely chopped*
3g fresh ginger, *peeled and finely chopped*
½ small fresh chilli, *finely chopped*
630g canned Italian whole peeled tomatoes
1 cup vegetable stock
¼ cup sugar
1½ tbsp fish sauce
1 bay leaf
50ml malt vinegar

1 litre canola oil
6 x 250g portions sirloin steak
3 tbsp Pukara extra-virgin olive oil
salt

onion rings

Separate the sliced onions evenly into 1cm rings. Soak in the milk for 2–3 hours. Spread out the breadcrumbs on an oven tray. Remove the rings from the milk and drain. Dust the rings with flour, then dip into the tempura batter, coating well, and lastly dip into the breadcrumbs. Place in the freezer until frozen.

kasundi

Heat the olive oil to a shimmer in a large saucepan. Once hot, add the fenugreek, mustard and cumin seeds and heat until they begin to pop. Add the turmeric and curry powders and cook for a further 30 seconds. Stir through the garlic, ginger and chilli and cook until soft. Add the tomatoes, stock, sugar, fish sauce, bay leaf and vinegar and cook until the tomatoes have broken down and a thick sauce is achieved.

assembly

Heat the canola oil in a medium-sized saucepan. When it has reached 185°C, carefully drop in the onion rings, four at a time, cooking them for about 3 minutes or until they turn golden. Repeat until all the onion rings are cooked, then set aside to keep warm.

Preheat the oven to 180°C. Season the steaks on both sides with olive oil and salt to taste. Heat a sauté pan then place the steaks, two at a time, into the pan and cook for 2 minutes per side. Transfer them to the oven for 6 minutes, remove from the oven and allow to rest for 5–8 minutes. Serve the steaks liberally covered with kasundi and 5–6 onion rings.

SERVES 6

SIMON SAYS *Always allow steak to reach room temperature prior to cooking. Heat the pan so it is as hot as possible — don't use a non-stick pan as it cannot be heated to the temperature needed without giving off undesirable fumes. Whenever possible use a cast-iron skillet, but don't oil it. Steak should always be seared on all sides.*

For rare steak, cook it over high heat until it reaches an internal temperature of 50°C, then remove it from the pan and leave to rest, covered. After 5–10 minutes measure the internal temperature with a meat thermometer; ideally it should be 60°C. If the steak is cooked to 60°C in the pan, the meat will continue to cook after removal and the result will be medium–rare meat. For medium steak, cook it until it reaches an internal temperature of 61°C, then rest as described above. When tested after 5–10 minutes, the temperature should have risen to 71°C. For well-done steak, cook until it reaches an internal temperature of 67°C, then leave it to rest until the temperature rises another 10°C. If the desired temperature is not reached, briefly sear the steak again on both sides then rest for another 5–10 minutes before checking the internal temperature.

HAVOC PORK, PARMA HAM & TRUFFLE HOLLANDAISE WITH MANCHEGO CHEESE BRIOCHE & BUTTER PUDDING

Havoc pork comes from a piggery in South Canterbury where the owner, Ian Jackson, free-range farms his animals. I was mystified by the name until I read of the occasion when the free-ranging pigs discovered and consumed a large amount of fallen and femented plums. With more than twice the breath alcohol limit for walking, even given two extra legs, the name Havoc seemed entirely appropriate.

For this recipe I have wrapped the Havoc pork in prosciutto. Salt-cured and air-dried Italian hams are mostly referred to simply as prosciutto, which is not entirely correct. Prosciutto is the Italian word for ham: if cured it is prosciutto crudo and if cooked, prosciutto cotto. The best of the cured Italian Prosciutto di Parma hams come from the little village of Langhirano, just south of Parma.

40g unsalted butter
1 small white onion, *finely diced*
1 medium clove garlic, *minced*
4 sage leaves, *finely chopped*
350ml cream
small pinch of allspice
small pinch of cinnamon
3 large eggs
200g brioche, *roughly diced, including crust*
80g Manchego cheese, *grated*
1 tsp salt
3 grinds of black pepper

brioche & butter pudding

Preheat the oven to 160°C. In a medium-sized saucepan, melt the butter over medium heat. Add the onion, garlic and sage, and cook for 7 minutes until the onion is transparent. Stir in the cream, allspice and cinnamon and bring to the boil. Remove from the heat and set aside to cool. In a medium to large bowl, whisk the eggs until well combined. Add the cooled cream mixture, whisking to incorporate, then fold in the diced brioche and leave to soak for 1 hour. Using a wooden spoon, mix until all the cream mixture is absorbed by the brioche. Fold in the grated cheese, salt and pepper. Spoon the mixture into the seven greased dariole moulds to 1cm from the top; gently tap each one on the bench to release any air that may be trapped. Choose a high-sided baking tray to use as a water bath for the puddings and add enough water to reach 2cm up around the moulds. Cover with tin foil and bake for 30 minutes or until the puddings start to swell slightly in the centre. Once cooked, remove from the water bath and set aside to cool. Remove the puddings from the moulds, place on a tray lined with baking paper and keep refrigerated until ready to reheat. (These puddings can be made the day before and refrigerated until needed.)

60ml white wine
60ml white vinegar
6 black peppercorns
2 bay leaves
200g unsalted butter
3 large egg yolks
pinch of black pepper
salt
1 tsp Dijon mustard
1 tsp Alba truffle paste
10ml white truffle oil

truffle hollandaise

In a small saucepan, bring the white wine, vinegar, peppercorns and bay leaves to the boil. Reduce by half, then set aside. Melt the butter in a medium-sized saucepan over a low heat. Remove the pan from the heat and set aside. Use a spoon to skim the foam off the surface of the butter and discard. Transfer the rest of the butter to a warmed pouring jug and set aside. In a bowl, whisk together the egg yolks and reduced white wine until frothy, then add the pepper, salt and mustard. Place the bowl over a saucepan of simmering water and whisk the egg yolks for 5 minutes or until they begin to thicken. Remove the bowl from the heat and continue to whisk the eggs for another minute to cool down (this is best done on a cold bench). Place the bowl with the eggs back over the saucepan, but not over heat. Very slowly pour the melted butter (leaving the milk solids behind) into the egg yolk mixture, whisking continuously. Finally, whisk in the truffle paste and truffle oil until thoroughly blended. Taste and adjust the seasoning.

900g or 3 large Havoc pork fillets, *cleaned and trimmed*
ground black pepper
12 thin slices Prosciutto di Parma

Havoc pork and Parma ham

Cut each pork fillet into two even pieces. Transfer to a tray and season with pepper. Lay out two slices of Parma ham so they overlap and are large enough to enclose one piece of fillet lengthways. Place a piece of fillet at one end and roll up tightly. Repeat this process with the remaining pork pieces, then place the wrapped pork onto a greased baking tray and set aside until ready to cook. Preheat the oven to 180°C. Bake the pork for 11 minutes. While the pork is still in the oven, reheat the puddings for 4 minutes. Remove the pork, setting it aside to rest while the puddings reheat for a further 5 minutes. Remove the puddings.

300ml Madeira jus *(see page 232)*
6 vine-ripened tomatoes, *oven roasted (see page 232)*
18 thin slices of truffle

special equipment 7 x 100ml dariole moulds

assembly

Heat the Madeira jus. Place a pudding slightly off centre on each plate and spoon the truffle hollandaise partially over each one. Cut the wrapped pork fillets into medallions and arrange on the plates around the puddings and hollandaise. Top each medallion with a slice of truffle, then drizzle 4 tablespoons of Madeira jus around the pork. Garnish with an oven-roasted tomato.

SERVES 6

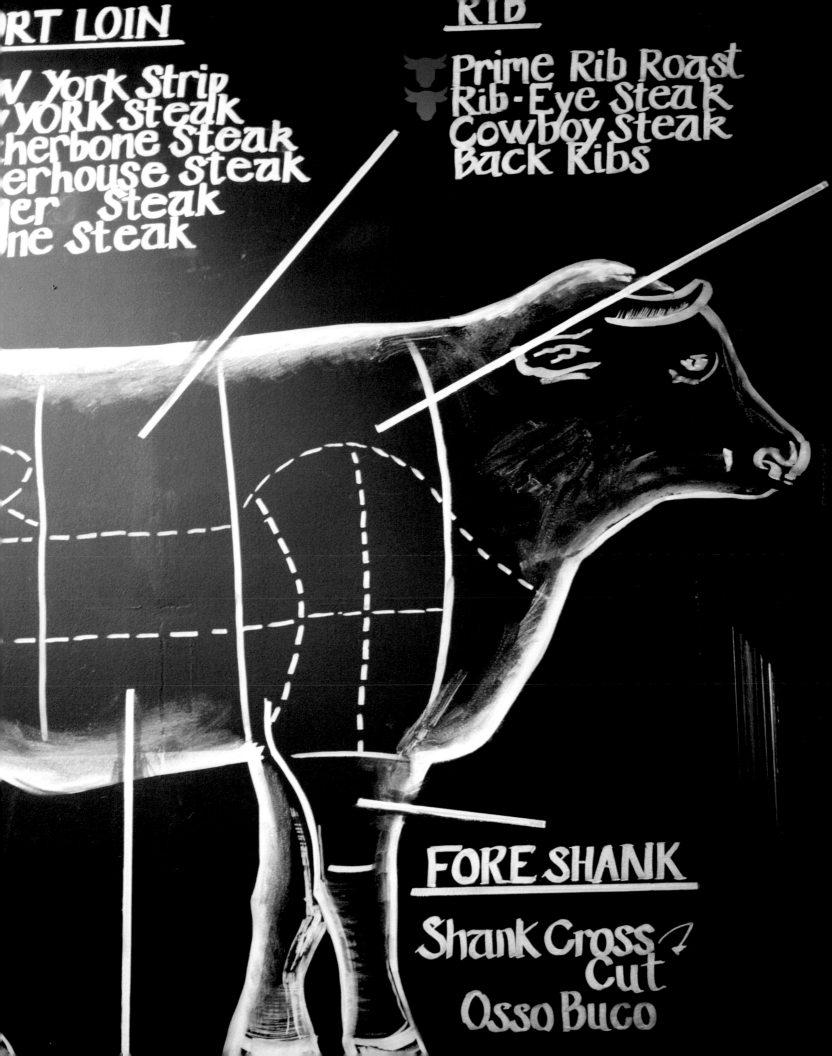

ANGUS PURE EYE FILLET WITH CIPOLLINE ONIONS & ARTICHOKE TOPPED WITH TRUFFLE MUSHROOM MASCARPONE

This dish is deceptively simple and therefore incredibly easy to get spectacularly wrong. Success hinges on the quality of the individual ingredients which, in combination and if correctly prepared, are sublime. Onions and artichokes in isolation probably wouldn't make headlines; nor will they in this dish if the wrong type are used. Artichokes preserved in brine never reheat well and are suited only to salad or antipasto presentations. The same goes for onions, particularly the cipolline onions used here; only use those that have been preserved in oil and lightly herbed.

9 artichokes, *preserved in oil*
12 cipolline onions, *preserved in oil*
6 fresh sprigs of thyme
6 tbsp Pukara extra-virgin olive oil
6 x 200g pieces Angus Pure eye fillet
salt and pepper

eye fillet

Preheat the oven to 220°C. Heat a grill or sauté pan until very hot. While the pan is heating, slice the artichokes in half, then place them flat-side down in the hot pan to colour and caramelise. Transfer to a baking tray. Add the cipolline onions and thyme sprigs to the tray and set aside. In a large frying pan, heat the olive oil to a shimmer and sauté each eye fillet for 10 seconds on each side. Transfer them to an oven dish, season with salt and pepper, then place in the oven for approximately 10 minutes or until the internal temperature is 60°C for rare, 71°C for medium and 77°C for well done. Allow the meat to rest for 8 minutes before serving. While the eye fillets are in the frying pan, heat the onions and artichokes in the oven.

150g mascarpone *(preferably Italian)*
2 tbsp finely chopped spring onion
2 tbsp mushroom truffle paste
　(see page 239 Crema Con Tartufo)
pinch of salt
2 grinds of black pepper

truffle mushroom mascarpone

In a bowl, mix together the mascarpone, spring onion, truffle paste and salt and pepper. Set aside.

6 sprigs of thyme
3 tbsp Malpighi Saporoso aged balsamic
　vinegar
2 tbsp Pukara extra-virgin olive oil

assembly

Arrange three pieces of artichoke and two onions on each plate. Slice each eye fillet in half across the grain and place onto the plate topped with a scoop of truffle mushroom mascarpone and a crisp sprig of thyme. Lastly, drizzle with balsamic and extra-virgin olive oil.

SIMON SAYS *Have you ever cooked steak at home and wondered why it never ends up quite as succulent and tender as it does in a restaurant? The secret lies in resting the meat; after cooking it — whether in the oven, pan or barbecue — place it on a warm (but not hot) plate and leave it to stand for up to 10 minutes and as much as 20 minutes for large pieces such as whole fillets or roasts. As the meat slowly cools down, the muscle fibres that have contracted during cooking start to relax and reabsorb the juices from the centre of the meat, drawing it back towards the edges. You will know if it has rested enough when the steak is cut; ideally the inside should be evenly moist.*

SERVES 6

HERB-CRUSTED ANGUS PURE RIB EYE WITH PORCINI MUSHROOMS & GREEN TOMATO SHERRY JUS

My grandfather could not abide rare meat. He was absolutely fanatical about it and would not even try a morsel. One evening at my parent's home, my father had prepared lamb on the barbecue and we, including my grandfather, were all enjoying it until some fool turned the lights up, revealing that the lamb was quite pink. That was the end of it for Grandpa: not another mouthful. No amount of remonstrating would convince him that the change in lighting could possibly have altered the lamb to the point where it was now inedible. The incident lent a whole new meaning to the saying 'being kept in the dark'.

2 tbsp olive oil

1 medium onion, *finely diced*

3 cloves garlic, *crushed*

½ small red chilli, *seeds removed and finely chopped*

3 sprigs of thyme, *finely chopped*

1 tbsp tomato paste

½ tsp salt

½ tsp pepper

150g salsa verde *(green tomato sauce see page 239 Salsa di Pomodori Verdi)*

250g can whole peeled tomatoes, *finely chopped*

200ml vegetable stock

250ml Madeira jus *(see page 232)*

100ml Tio Pepe sherry

250g cooked porcini mushrooms *(see page 238)*

3 x 600g pieces Angus Pure rib eye

2 pinches of herb salt

3 grinds of black pepper

100g Simon Gault herb rub *(see page 238)*

200g Parmigiano-Reggiano, *grated*

jus

In a medium-sized saucepan over medium heat, bring the oil to a shimmer. Add the onion, garlic, chilli and thyme and sauté for 6 minutes or until the onion is translucent. Add the tomato paste, salt, pepper, salsa verde, chopped tomatoes and vegetable stock. Bring to a simmer and cook for 5 minutes before adding the Madeira jus and the sherry. Simmer for a further 3 minutes. Add the porcini mushrooms to heat through, check the seasoning and adjust as required. Set aside and keep warm.

assembly

Preheat the oven to 200°C. Heat a large frying pan over a high heat and sear each rib eye on both sides until golden (this could also be done on a barbecue for added flavour). Season each rib eye with the herb salt and pepper, then place the meat on an oven tray and rub each side with Simon Gault herb rub. Place in the oven and cook for approximately 10–12 minutes until done. (Medium is best for this cut, i.e. an internal temperature of 68°C. The cooking time will vary depending on the size of the cut of meat used. As always, a meat thermometer is the most reliable means of avoiding embarrassing incinerations.) Once the meat is cooked to your liking, change the setting on the oven from bake to grill and sprinkle the meat with the grated cheese. Grill until golden, then allow the meat to rest for 7–10 minutes. Slice each rib eye out from the bone and divide the meat between six plates. Finish with the green tomato sherry jus.

SERVES 6

ROTISSERIE MERINO CROSS LEG OF LAMB WITH ROASTED VEGETABLES & A CHOCOLATE BALSAMIC JUS

This is a simple but classic New Zealand leg of lamb recipe. When buying lamb at today's prices one needs to make every dollar count, so I use only merino cross lamb from the Central Otago high country. Raised on natural tussock and aromatic herb pastures, in my view this lamb is the best available.

2 tender sprigs of rosemary

leaves from 4 stalks of thyme *(discard stalks)*

2 cloves garlic

½ cup Pukara extra-virgin olive oil

1 tsp cayenne pepper

1 tsp salt

herb oil

Finely chop the herbs, then place with the rest of the ingredients in a blender and process until smooth. Set aside until required.

3 tbsp salted butter

1 medium clove garlic, *minced*

6 large portobello mushrooms

½ eggplant, *cut into 6 strips lengthways*

1½ courgettes, *cut into quarters lengthways*

salt and cracked black pepper

1 red capsicum, *cut in half and deseeded*

vegetables

Preheat the oven to 180°C. Melt the butter and add the minced garlic. Place the mushrooms and the prepared eggplant and courgette on an oven tray, season with salt and pepper, brush with garlic butter and roast for 10 minutes. Remove from the oven and set aside. Increase the oven temperature to 220°C. Place the capsicum on a greased oven tray, skin-side up, and roast for 10 minutes. Remove and allow to cool in a bowl covered with cling film or in a plastic ziplock bag. Once cool, remove as much skin as possible, then cut each half into three strips lengthways.

1kg tunnel-boned lamb leg

salt and cracked black pepper

lamb

Using a sharp boning or filleting knife, cut along the lamb where the bone has been removed to trim any excess fat and sinew. Season the lamb with the salt and cracked pepper. Rub half the herb oil into the lamb and roll it up, skin-side out. Using cooking string, truss the lamb to restore it to its original shape ready for threading onto the rotisserie skewer. Season the exterior of the parcel and spear it with the rotisserie skewer as close to the centre as you can. Cook, basting occasionally with the remaining herb oil, until the internal temperature measured in the centre of the meat is 58°C. Remove the meat from the rotisserie and rest in a warm area for 30 minutes (it will not harm it to let it rest even longer, perhaps while you enjoy a first course).

180ml Madeira jus *(see page 232)*

6 tsp chocolate balsamic vinegar

jus

Place the Madeira jus in a jug and add the chocolate balsamic vinegar. Mix well to combine.

6 vine-ripened tomatoes

6 semi-dried tomatoes

assembly

Preheat the oven to 220°C. Roast the vine tomatoes as described in the method on page 232. Reheat the vegetables and the jus. Slice the lamb. Arrange the roasted vegetables, including a tomato, on each plate, then add some sliced lamb. Place a semi-dried tomato on top of the lamb, then pour some chocolate balsamic jus to one side.

special equipment *meat thermometer*

SERVES 6

SIMON SAYS *Before cooking any meat, remove it from the refrigerator and allow it to approach room temperature, covered. If roasting meat rather than using a rotisserie, use a roasting rack to ensure even browning and heat circulation. The amount of fat on the lamb leg and the fattiness of the leg will determine the cooking time and temperature. For a lean leg, have the oven at 230°C for the first 15 minutes and then reduce it to 175°C for the remainder of the time. Using this method, the meat will take about 25 minutes per 450g to reach medium rare. Fattier cuts of meat are better roasted at a lower temperature; 160°C will allow the fat to slowly melt and baste the roast. Meat cooked like this will take about 30 minutes per 450g to reach medium rare. The most accurate way to determine doneness is with a meat thermometer: 42°C is rare, 58°C is medium rare (my preference), and 68°C is medium–well done. Always rest the roast after cooking for at least 15 minutes before slicing to retain the moistness.*

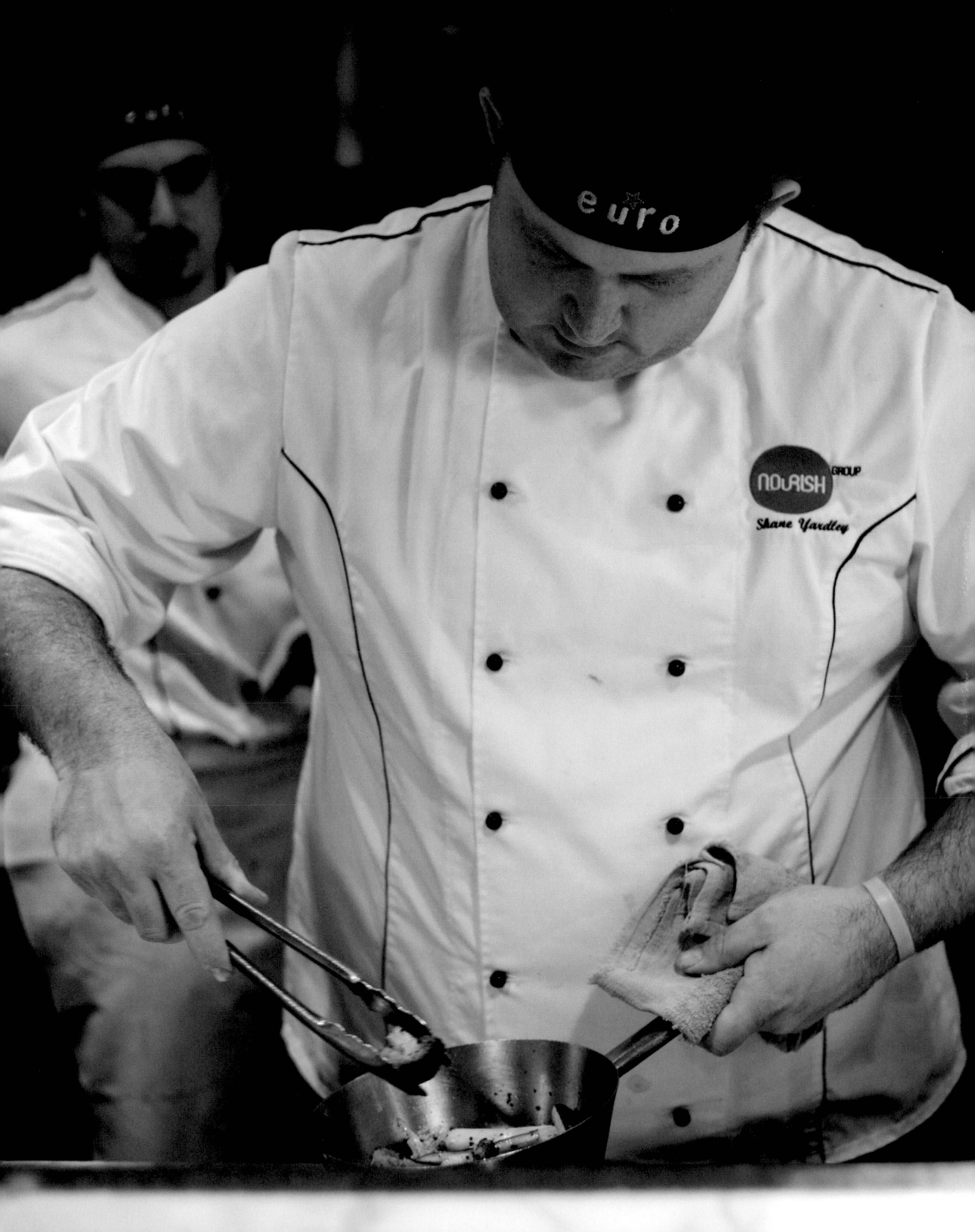
euro
NOURISH GROUP
Shane Yardley

BLACK ANGUS PIE WITH LEMON PROSCIUTTO DUMPLINGS

I am tempted to call this 'Herbert Pie' in recognition of one of my favourite Euro customers. This gentleman is a regular luncheon visitor and as soon as he is seated we put the Black Angus pie in the oven for him. We have yet to get it wrong. Inevitably he will catch us out, but in the short term we will continue to prepare the pie. On the day he doesn't confirm the order I think the sensible and caring option would be to summon an ambulance. He will need it or, failing that, it will be required for the chef who ruined his last pie.

100ml olive oil
2 medium onions, *diced*
1 medium carrot, *diced*
1 stalk celery, *diced*
6 cloves garlic, *crushed and finely chopped*
handful of fresh thyme, *finely chopped*
900g diced rib eye
50g plain flour
1 tbsp tomato paste
1 cup Marsala
1 tsp salt
8 grinds of pepper
1 litre beef stock
750ml water
2 tbsp Worcestershire sauce

225g pork cheek mince
125g Prosciutto di Parma, *minced or finely chopped*
zest of ½ a lemon
2 tbsp chopped parsley
large pinch of salt
4 grinds of black pepper

580g plain flour
1 tsp salt
290g cold butter, *cut into 1cm dice*
130ml ice-cold water

1 egg yolk and 2 tbsp milk, *mixed*
6 tbsp mascarpone
2 slices Prosciutto di Parma, *finely diced*
1 spring onion, *sliced into a fine julienne*

special equipment *6 x 300ml pie dishes*

filling

In a medium-sized saucepan, heat half the oil over medium heat until shimmering. Add the prepared vegetables and herbs. Cook, stirring, for 8 minutes until the onion is golden brown. Transfer the contents of the pan to a bowl and set aside. Using the same saucepan over medium–high heat, add the remaining oil and heat until shimmering. Add the beef and cook for 5–8 minutes, stirring so it doesn't catch, until the meat begins to brown. Return the vegetables to the pan and add the flour, stirring for 1 minute, then add the tomato paste, Marsala, salt and pepper. Continue stirring and cook for a further minute, then add the stock, water and Worcestershire sauce. Lower the heat and simmer for 1½–2 hours until the meat is tender and the sauce has thickened.
Set aside to cool.

dumplings

While the pie filling is simmering, prepare the dumplings. Mix together all the ingredients, then roll into 24 small balls. (To achieve even-sized balls, simply divide the mix in half, then divide each half into three. Divide each of the six pieces into quarters and set aside.)

shortcrust pastry

Place the flour in a food processor, then on medium speed add the salt and blend for 1 minute. Add the butter, a few pieces at a time, until it has all been incorporated and the mixture has a sandy texture. Slowly pour in the ice-cold water until a soft dough ball starts to form. Remove the dough and place on a cold, hard surface. Using your hands, mould it into a ball, then divide it into six equal pieces. Place each piece between two sheets of greaseproof paper and roll out to a thickness of 3–4mm.

assembly

Preheat the oven to 180°C. Spoon the cooled meat filling into the individual pie dishes to fill to two-thirds. Top with four dumplings. Arrange the pastry over the top of the dumplings and cut off any excess from around the edge of the dish. Bake the pies for 10 minutes then brush the pie tops with the egg wash and return them to the oven for 15–20 minutes more until golden brown. Combine the mascarpone and prosciutto and serve each pie with a tablespoon of mascarpone, dressed with spring onion. Serve with a selection of roasted vegetables.

SERVES 6

VENISON CRUSTED WITH JUNIPER & ORANGE ON FENNEL & ONION WITH CITRUS JUS

New Zealand is the main source of farm-raised venison for the world market and the meat is lower in calories, cholesterol and fat than most cuts of beef, pork or lamb. For me there are only two options when serving venison, rare or casseroled, and of the two I far prefer the former. There are claims made that deer antler velvet is a natural health supplement and that it helps in maintaining joint mobility. My father has been taking deer velvet tablets for some time now but we haven't seen any real improvement, though we are encouraging him to stop trying to jump the farm fences and use the gates.

crust

2 oranges
1 tbsp black peppercorns
1 tbsp green peppercorns
1 tbsp pink peppercorns
½ tbsp juniper berries
960g venison short loin fillet, *trimmed and cut into 6 pieces*
1 tsp flaky salt

Preheat the oven to 100°C. With a citrus zester, remove the zest from the two oranges in 5cm lengths. Blanch twice in boiling water for 1 minute, each time using fresh water. Place the blanched zest on baking paper or a Teflon sheet and dry for 1 hour in the oven until hard. Once the zest is dried, use a pestle and mortar to crush it along with the peppercorns and juniper berries. Sieve the mixture, discarding the fine powder and retaining the coarse orange pepper mixture. Put 1½ teaspoons of the mixture aside to be used in the sauce. Season each piece of vension with the salt then lightly coat each piece in the remaining spice mixture. Wrap each piece tightly in cling film and refrigerate overnight.

vegetables

280g fennel bulbs
3 tbsp Pukara extra-virgin olive oil
salt and pepper
250g courgettes
6 cipolline onions, *preserved in oil*

Preheat the oven to 180°C. Cut the fennel into small wedges. Transfer to a bowl with one-third of the oil, season with salt and pepper and mix together. Place the coated fennel on a baking tray and roast for 8 minutes. Meanwhile, cut the courgettes into 5cm lengths, then lengthways into quarters, and cut the onions in half. Place in the bowl used for the fennel and add the rest of the oil and seasonings. Place the prepared courgettes and onion in the oven with the fennel and roast for 8 minutes. Keep warm.

venison

2 tbsp Pukara extra-virgin olive oil

300ml Madeira jus *(see page 232)*
6 tbsp orange and onion salsa *(Salsarancia Cipolle see page 239)*

special equipment *citrus zester, pestle and mortar*

Preheat the oven to 180°C. Remove the venison from the refrigerator and unwrap, but keep covered while it reaches room temperature. Heat the olive oil in a large frying pan until shimmering, then seal the meat — two pieces at a time — by searing it in the oil until an even caramel colour is achieved on all sides. Transfer the meat to a roasting pan and place in the oven. Roast until the desired cooking temperature is reached: about 3–4 minutes for rare. Once cooked, leave to rest. Pour off any oil left in the pan and add the meat juices to the Madeira jus. Add the orange and onion salsa and 1½ teaspoons of the orange pepper spice to the sauce. Keep warm.

assembly

Slice the meat on an angle and fan it out onto each plate. Place the roasted vegetables on the meat. Finish with the sauce and serve any additional sauce separately.

SERVES 6

BLACK PEPPER RAGOÛT OF LAMB ON WILD ONION RISOTTO WITH ONION RINGS

This dish is always better made a day in advance to allow the flavours to mature and intensify. Preparing it in advance then reheating it has obvious time-saving advantages as well. Even the onion rings can be made earlier and frozen for later use.

1.2kg boned lamb leg
6 cloves garlic
150ml Pukara extra-virgin olive oil
150g carrots, *roughly diced*
250g onions, *roughly diced*
100g celery, *roughly diced*
2 tbsp tomato paste
3 tsp salt
150g plain flour
300ml red wine
2.2 litres vegetable stock
30g black peppercorns
4 sprigs of thyme
2 sprigs of rosemary

1.2 litre vegetable stock
50g butter
3 tbsp Pukara extra-virgin olive oil
1 medium white onion, *finely diced*
2 cloves garlic, *minced*
1½ cups Arborio rice
175ml white wine
8 cipolline onions preserved in oil, *roughly chopped*
80g Parmigiano-Reggiano, *grated*
salt and pepper

50g horseradish cream
200g Japanese breadcrumbs
2 tsp salt flakes
½ tsp ground white pepper
2 large onions
500ml milk
180g flour
200ml tempura batter *(see page 233)*

1 litre canola oil for frying
rocket *(arugula)*

lamb ragoût

Cut the lamb leg into 2.5cm dice. With the back of a knife, crush the garlic cloves and remove the outer husk. Pour one-third of the oil into a large casserole dish and heat to a shimmer. Add the garlic and vegetables and sauté over a medium heat for 6–7 minutes until they start to brown. Add the tomato paste and cook for a further 3 minutes. Remove from the heat and set aside. Add the salt to the flour. In a large sauté pan, heat the remaining oil to a shimmer. Lightly dust half the diced lamb in the flour and sauté for 5 minutes until golden brown, turning the pieces regularly so that the lamb browns evenly on all sides. Repeat the process with the remaining lamb. Add the red wine, stock, peppercorns, thyme, rosemary and sautéed vegetables. Cover and simmer for 1½ hours or until the lamb is tender.

risotto

In a medium-sized saucepan, bring the stock and butter to the boil and turn off the heat. In a larger saucepan, heat the olive oil and sauté the white onion and garlic over a low heat until transparent. Add the rice and sauté for 3 minutes, stirring continuously with a wooden spoon. Add the white wine and stir over a medium heat until the rice absorbs the wine. Add half a cup of the hot stock and butter mixture, stirring to ensure the rice does not catch. When the liquid has been absorbed, add another half cup of the stock. Keep adding the stock, stirring continuously until only half a cup remains. At this point add the chopped cipolline onions. The process should take 25–35 minutes and the rice should be al dente. Add the grated cheese, stirring to incorporate, and season with salt and pepper.

onion rings

Mix the horseradish cream with the breadcrumbs and add salt and pepper. Slice the onions evenly into 1cm thick slices and separate into single rings. Soak the rings in the milk for 2–3 hours. Pat the rings dry and dust in the flour, then dip them into the tempura batter to evenly coat. Dip the rings in the breadcrumb mixture. Place the coated rings on a tray lined with baking paper and freeze until required.

assembly

Reheat the lamb over a medium heat until piping hot. Pour the canola oil into a large saucepan and heat to 170°C. Cook the onion rings in batches until golden brown. Drain on paper towels and keep warm until ready to use. Divide the risotto and lamb between six large plates. Top each plate with a stack of four onion rings and arrange the rocket so that it appears to be sprouting out of the onion rings.

SERVES 6

ROASTED LAMB FILLET IN PARMA HAM WITH ARMAGNAC & PRUNE JUS, BRAISED LETTUCE & PEAS

This is a menu item from our Pravda restaurant in Wellington. The salty sweetness of the prosciutto wrapping subtly flavours the lamb and the roasted capsicum centre complements the two meats perfectly. Roasting capsicums produces a superb, almost smoky flavour and it is important to really blacken the skins to extract the maximum effect. Capsicum flesh contains so much water that it is almost impossible to overdo the roasting. The trick of bagging the capsicum after roasting makes removing the very thin and often stubborn skin much easier.

jus

55g prunes, *pitted*
120ml Armagnac
300ml Madeira jus *(see page 232)*

Thinly slice the prunes and place in a saucepan with the Armagnac. Over a medium–high heat (take care if cooking on gas of the flame that may result), reduce by half to remove the strong alcohol flavour. Add the Madeira jus to finish. Set aside until required.

roasted lamb

1 red capsicum
10ml Pukara extra-virgin olive oil
¼ tsp flaky salt
6 x 180g portions lamb fillet
12 slices Prosciutto di Parma
¼ tsp flaky salt
¼ tsp freshly ground black pepper
1 tbsp Pukara extra-virgin olive oil

Preheat the oven to 200°C. Slice the capsicum in half from top to bottom and remove all seeds. Rub with olive oil and a little salt then place on an oven tray skin-side up. Roast for 12–15 minutes or until the skin begins to blister. Remove from the oven and place in a ziplock bag or a bowl and seal it with the lid or cling film. When cooled, remove the skin from the capsicum and slice the flesh from top to bottom, creating long strips. Cut the lamb fillets in half and place a strip of capsicum between the two halves. Lay a slice of prosciutto flat on a chopping board, taking care not to tear it. Place the lamb stack at one end and roll to encase it. Repeat to create rolled packages. Season each with the second measure of salt and the pepper. Heat the olive oil until shimmering in a sauté pan, then add the rolls and seal. Transfer them to an oven dish and cook for 3 minutes on both sides or until an internal temperature of 55°C is reached. Remove from the oven and allow to rest in a warm place for 5 minutes.

braised lettuce

½ iceberg lettuce
½ savoy cabbage
175ml chicken stock *(see page 230)*
120g green peas *(fresh or frozen)*
30g butter
½ clove garlic, *minced*

Discard dark coloured outer leaves from the lettuce and cabbage. Separate the lettuce and 12 of the cabbage leaves and remove the central ribs. Keeping the lettuce and cabbage leaves separate, stack each and slice into long thin strips. In a large saucepan, reduce the chicken stock by half, add the cabbage and cook for 2 minutes. Add the butter, lettuce, peas and minced garlic. Stir to combine and coat with butter, then remove from the heat. This must be served immediately so timing is important. Taste and season.

assembly

1 tsp white truffle oil

Arrange the drained lettuce and peas in the centre of the plate. Slice the lamb in half on a 45° angle and place on top of the lettuce. Spoon the prune and Armagnac jus on and around the lamb, and drizzle truffle oil over the top.

SERVES 6

GRILLED BLUENOSE WITH COURGETTES & GREEN PEA SALSA VERDE

Bluenose warehou is a species of fish gaining popularity with chefs partly because, I suspect, we seem to have eaten almost everything else available. The bluenose hunts over the rocky bottom and around the reefs on the coast of both the North and South islands. Individual fish can weigh up to around 35kg; its firm flesh that caramelises beautifully when grilled, makes it a prized catch. Its very large eyes suggest great underwater visual acuity but its much lived in blunt nose seems to indicate that it may have experienced repeated high-speed collisions with the home-town reef. The reality is that most diners have little interest in piscatorial beauty pageants once the fish hits the plate — and anyway, those repeated collisions could well have contributed to the superb density of the flesh!

1 cup green peas
¼ cup basil leaves
¼ cup parsley
¼ cup mint
¼ cup oregano
½ cup Pukara extra-virgin olive oil
1 tbsp capers
2 good-quality anchovy fillets

6 x 180–200g bluenose fillets, *skinned and cut into 12 pieces*
salt and pepper
1 tbsp chopped parsley
1 tbsp Pukara extra-virgin olive oil
2 tbsp unsalted butter

1 tbsp Pukara extra-virgin olive oil
500g diced courgettes
100g baby spinach
salt and pepper

1 lime, *cut into 6 wedges*

salsa verde
Bring a saucepan of salted water to the boil and cook the peas for 3 minutes; they should remain bright green. Run the peas under cold running water to stop the cooking process. Place the fresh herbs, olive oil, capers and anchovies in a food processor and process until well combined and smooth. Mix into the peas and set aside.

bluenose
Season the fish fillets with salt, pepper and chopped parsley. Bring a large sauté pan to a moderate heat, add the extra-virgin olive oil and heat until shimmering. Place the butter in the pan and then the fish directly on top. Cook for 3–4 minutes on each side, depending on the thickness of the fish. Remove and keep warm. If the pan is not large enough it may be necessary to cook the fish in two batches.

courgettes
Heat the oil over a moderate heat and sauté the courgettes for 4 minutes. Add the spinach leaves, along with the green pea salsa verde and toss together in the pan for another 1 minute. Season with salt and pepper.

assembly
Divide the courgettes evenly between six plates, place two fish fillets on top of each serving and garnish with a wedge of lime so the diners can squeeze the juice over the fish to enhance its flavour.

SIMON SAYS *A basic guideline for cooking fish is 8 minutes per 2.5cm of thickness, but in reality everyone uses a different cooking temperature. Then, to add to the confusion, fish is like meat in that it continues to cook after you remove it from the heat source. Overcooked fish borders on food vandalism, but can so easily be prevented. Use the tip of a small knife to divide the flesh and inspect the interior. Do not cook the fish until it flakes; this is too long. Once the flesh show signs of firming and is starting to go from translucent to opaque, the cooking process is complete. If cooking fish on the bone, the flesh should lightly resist pulling away from the bone.*

SERVES 6

FILLET OF SNAPPER WITH ALASKAN KING CRAB RATATOUILLE & CARROT & GINGER BEURRE BLANC

Ratatouille is usually served as a side dish, but it may also be served alone in its own right. First time around, use it in this main course and the next day as a light luncheon. During summer, it can be served as a cold main course dish. It keeps for several days in the refrigerator unless, of course, as in this case, it contains crab or some other more perishable embellishment. Ratatouille is great served with couscous or rice; all in all it's a superb rescue package for feeding unexpected guests. The carrot and ginger beurre blanc is also versatile and very good with chicken and asparagus.

ratatouille

90ml Pukara extra-virgin olive oil

¼ medium onion, *finely diced*

1 clove garlic, *minced*

2 x 350g eggplants, *peeled and chopped into 1cm cubes*

110g courgette, *chopped into 1cm cubes*

1 red capsicum, *seeds removed, cored and roughly diced*

250ml tomato sauce *(see page 233)*

1 sprig of thyme

1 tbsp tomato paste

1 tsp vegetable stock powder

salt

cracked black pepper

6 basil leaves, torn

200g Alaskan red king crab meat, *removed from shell and diced*

In a saucepan, heat the olive oil to a shimmer and sauté the onion and garlic for 3 minutes until translucent. Add the eggplant, courgette and capsicum and sauté for a further 4 minutes. Add the tomato sauce and cook, stirring, for 2 minutes, then add the thyme, tomato paste and stock powder. Bring to a simmer for 3 minutes. Season with salt and pepper to taste and allow the mixture to cool before adding the basil and half the crab meat, reserving the balance for garnish.

carrot purée

120g carrot, *diced*

1 tsp sugar

1 tsp salt

cracked black pepper

Place the carrot in cold water. Add the salt and sugar and bring to the simmer. Cook until soft (approximately 20 minutes). Strain off the water and purée the carrot until silky smooth in a food processor. Set aside.

beurre blanc

20g fresh ginger, *roughly chopped*

1 shallot, *thinly sliced*

1 clove garlic, *thinly sliced*

90ml white wine

90ml white wine vinegar

1 bay leaf

3 whole black peppercorns

150ml cream

150g unsalted butter, *cubed and chilled*

Place the ginger, shallot and garlic in a saucepan with the white wine, white wine vinegar, bay leaf and peppercorns. Reduce until about 1 tablespoon remains. Add the cream and continue to reduce over a medium–low heat until about 100ml (6–8 tbsp) of the mixture remains. Remove from the heat and slowly whisk in the cold butter, piece by piece. When half the butter cubes have been stirred in, the cubes can be added two at a time. Continue stirring until all the butter has been added and the sauce thickens — do not allow the sauce to boil at any time. Season with the salt and pepper, then pass through a fine sieve. Mix with the carrot purée and set aside to keep warm in a thermos flask or a jug in a bowl of warm water until required.

6 vine-riped tomatoes, *roasted*
  (see page 232)
1.2kg snapper fillets
salt
cracked black pepper
plain flour
50ml Pukara extra-virgin olive oil
150g unsalted butter
6 sprigs of chervil

assembly

Preheat the oven to 180°C. Place the roasted tomatoes in the oven to reheat. Season the snapper with salt and pepper and dust lightly in the flour, patting off any excess. In a large sauté pan, heat half the olive oil until shimmering, then add half the butter. (It won't be possible or desirable to fit all the fish in the pan at once so cook it in two batches.) Place half the snapper fillets into the pan skin-side down. Once the fish has turned a golden-brown colour (about 30 seconds), flip it over using a fish slice and cook the other side until it is also golden brown. Transfer to an oven tray lined with tin foil. Pour over the pan juices. Clean the pan and repeat the process with the remaining fish fillets. Transfer the fish to the oven and bake for 2–3 minutes. Check that the fish is cooked by inspecting the centre: the inside should be lighter in colour and easy to flake.

While the fish is cooking reheat the ratatouille. Spoon the sauce onto serving plates. Use the back of a spoon to spread the carrot and ginger beurre blanc into an attractive design. Divide the ratatouille equally between the plates, top with the remaining crab and garnish with a sprig of chervil. Place a piece of the fish and a roasted tomato on each plate.

SERVES 6

AKAROA SALMON & HAVOC PORK BELLY WITH TRUFFLE CREAMED SAVOY CABBAGE & APPLE CIDER GASTRIQUE

With the popularity of pork belly on restaurant menus it is surprising that there is any available for streaky bacon or Asian cooking. In this recipe I have brought together the products of two New Zealand South Island farmers: Akaroa salmon is farmed, not surprisingly, in the Akaroa Harbour and Havoc pork, as already mentioned, is grown in South Canterbury. Salmon and pork may seem an odd combination but no more so than crayfish (lobster) and steak, or bacon and eggs for that matter. These two do in fact balance each other nicely.

½ cup rock salt
10 whole cardamom pods
5 bay leaves, *cut into small pieces*
15 whole black peppercorns
10 pink or green peppercorns
10 whole cloves
2 cinnamon sticks, *broken into bits*
1.2kg piece pork belly
1 large onion, *thickly sliced*
1 large carrot, *sliced lengthways*

pork belly

In a food processor, blend together the salt, cardamom, bay leaves, peppercorns, cloves and cinnamon. Rub this mixture on both sides of the pork belly, then place the meat on a tray and refrigerate for 7 hours or overnight. Rinse the pork under cold water then score the skin with a very sharp knife at 5mm intervals, penetrating just through the skin. Place the pork in a large saucepan and cover with cold water. Bring to the boil, then remove the pork from the water. Place the chopped onion and carrot on a baking tray with the pork belly resting skin-side up on top of the vegetables. Preheat the oven to 180°C. Roast for between 1¾–2 hours depending on the thickness or until the scored skin is crispy and golden. When cooked, the meat should easily pull apart. Set aside until ready to use.

25g caster sugar
100ml cider
50ml white wine vinegar
½ Granny Smith apple, *skinned, peeled and finely diced*
150ml Madeira jus *(see page 232)*

apple cider gastrique

Caramelise the sugar with 2 tablespoons of water over a low–medium heat, taking care that it does not burn. Add the cider and vinegar. Simmer for 5 minutes, stirring to dissolve the sugar. Add the apple and Madeira jus. Set aside.

½ savoy cabbage
250ml cream
1 tbsp black truffle paste or 1 medium white or black truffle, *finely diced*
salt
ground black pepper

creamed savoy cabbage

Trim the stalks and thinly slice the cabbage leaves. In a large saucepan of boiling salted water, blanch the cabbage until soft. Rinse under cold running water and drain. In a medium saucepan, bring the cream to the boil. Add the truffle paste or diced truffle and simmer until the bubbles start to slow and the mixture begins to thicken. Add the cabbage, season with salt and pepper, then set aside.

1 small side of salmon, *skin on, boned and cut into 6 portions*
salt, *preferably herb salt if available*
2 tbsp olive oil

assembly

Preheat the oven to 180°C. Season both sides of the salmon with salt. In a large ovenproof frying pan, heat the oil until it begins to shimmer. Place the salmon, skin-side down, into the pan and immediately transfer it to the oven for 6–8 minutes. The salmon flesh will lighten in colour when it is cooked. While the salmon is cooking, reheat the pork, cabbage and gastrique sauce. Cut the pork belly into six even pieces. Place one at one end of each hot plate and a serving of the creamed cabbage at the other end. Top the cabbage with a piece of salmon, then finish by saucing the pork belly with the gastrique.

SERVES 6

GRILLED HAPUKA WITH SAUTÉED BABY SQUID, POTATO GNOCCHI & MUSSEL SAUCE SCENTED WITH SHERRY

North of New Zealand's Bombay hills this fish is known as hapuka, while to the south it's groper. If you think that's confusing, consider how mixed up the poor fish must be: the young of the species are predominantly female i.e. initially they are girl fish (or is that mermaids?) then, at about 10–12kg, they turn into males. Arthur or Martha, hapuka or groper — they are a great eating fish. I use a little Tio Pepe fine sherry with this dish, but as the assembly comes together rather abruptly I would not recommend any testing of the quality of the sherry during this time. However, if one can resist sampling, their abstinence will be well rewarded.

300ml white wine
10 medium-sized green-lipped mussels
juice and zest of ½ a lime
300ml fresh cream
pinch of white pepper

mussel sauce

Heat 100ml of the wine in a lidded saucepan, add the mussels and cook until the mussels open; discard any that do not open. Remove from the wine and cool. Remove any beards, the brown foot and muscles that are attached to the shell. Cut each mussel into 3 or 4 pieces and set aside. In a clean saucepan combine the remaining wine, lime juice and zest; reduce by half. Add the cream and further reduce to leave 1 cup. Add the mussel meat and a pinch of white pepper. Set aside.

2 tbsp Pukara extra-virgin olive oil
6 x 150g pieces hapuka
salt
ground black pepper
2 tbsp unsalted butter

grilled hapuka

Massage the olive oil into the pieces of fish and season. Heat a large pan until hot, place the butter into the pan and lay the fish on top of the butter, skin-side up. Reduce the heat of the pan slightly to avoid burning the butter. Cook for approximately 3–4 minutes, carefully turn the fish and cook for a further 3–4 minutes. Spoon the butter over the presentation side of the fish to enhance the flavour and prevent the fish from drying out. When cooked place on paper towel and keep warm.

20ml Pukara extra-virgin olive oil
200g baby squid tubes
¼ tsp flaky salt
200g cooked gnocchi *(see page 231)*
15ml Tio Pepe dry sherry
150g baby spinach leaves
3 tbsp finely chopped chives

assembly

In a sauté pan, heat the olive oil to a shimmer. Add the baby squid and sprinkle with salt. Sauté over a high heat for 40–60 seconds — no longer — then transfer it to a sieve, discarding any liquid. In the same pan, heat the gnocchi with the mussel sauce. When the gnocchi is hot, add the sherry and baby spinach. Bring to a simmer, add the chives and adjust the seasoning as required. Stir well so the ingredients are well distributed through the sauce. Just before serving, add the cooked squid to warm through. Place the pieces of fish onto warmed plates, slightly off centre. Spoon the sauce over and beside the fish, leaving part of it exposed to make an attractive contrast of colours and textures.

SIMON SAYS *To clean the baby squid tubes, simply cut off the head and remove the filling from the tube or body. Don't forget to remove the plastic-like backbone of the squid — it can be felt within the tube during the gutting operation. Rinse the tubes under cold water. Better still, get your fishmonger to do all this for you.*

SERVES 6

STEAMED PRAWNS WITH WILTED SPINACH & PORK BELLY ON SPICY PORCINI JUS

This is an Italian-inspired dish that began its evolution at a Saturday morning market in a Tuscan village. It is very common to find a stall at these markets that offers roasted pork. The pig is roasted whole, generally over a wood fire; it is heavily salted and seasoned with garlic, rosemary and a good deal of fennel, along with other herbs. I first purchased some slices of this porchetta, as it is called, to have for my evening meal. It smelt so good I had to sample it but found it way too salty for me so when it came time to prepare the meal I added the fresh wilted spinach. The combination worked well, particularly with the acidity of the lemon juice. Since that time prawns have found their way into the ingredient list and the pork has become the belly cut.

¼ cup rock salt
5 whole cardamom pods
2 bay leaves, *cut into small pieces*
8 whole black peppercorns
5 pink peppercorns
5 whole cloves
1 cinnamon stick, *broken into pieces*
600g piece pork belly
1 large carrot, *roughly chopped*
1 large onion, *roughly chopped*

pork belly

In a food processor, blend together the salt, cardamom, bay leaves, peppercorns, cloves and cinnamon, then rub this on both sides of the pork belly. Place the meat on a tray and refrigerate for 7 hours or overnight. Rinse the pork belly under cold water, pat dry, then score the skin lengthways with a very sharp knife at 5mm intervals to just penetrate the skin. Place the meat in a large saucepan and cover with cold water. Bring to the boil, then remove from the water. Place the chopped carrot and onion on a baking tray with the pork belly resting skin-side up on top of the vegetables. Preheat the oven to 180°C. Roast in the oven for 2 hours until the scored skin becomes crispy and golden or until the pork is very tender. When it is done, the meat should easily pull apart. Set aside until ready to use.

18 medium-sized prawn tails, *shelled*
1 lemon, *sliced*

steamed prawns

Insert a bamboo skewer lengthways into each of 12 prawns to stop them from curling as they are steamed. Fill the steamer base with 4cm of hot water, add the sliced lemon, then bring to the boil. Place all the prawns into the steamer and cook for a few minutes; the time will vary from steamer to steamer but it should take about 4–6 minutes.

300ml Madeira jus *(see page 232)*
5 tbsp porcini paste *(see page 239 Crema di Funghi Porcini)*
1 small fresh hot chilli, *finely sliced*
15g salted butter

jus

In a saucepan, heat the Madeira jus with the porcini paste and chilli. Once it has come to the boil, whisk in the butter. Reheat just prior to serving.

20ml Pukara extra-virgin olive oil
300g washed spinach
juice of 1 lemon
large pinch of salt

assembly

Preheat the oven to 180°C. Reheat the pork belly, skin-side up. In a sauté pan, heat the oil to a shimmer, add the spinach and cook for about 1 minute. Add the lemon juice and season the contents of the pan with salt. Place the spinach on warmed plates. Slice the pork into six pieces and arrange them on the spinach. Remove the prawns from the steamer and arrange one curled tail and two straight tails on each plate. Pour the hot sauce onto the plate, but not over the pork or spinach.

special equipment, *steamer, 12x 10cm bamboo skewers*

SIMON SAYS *Hang the meat in the refrigerator, uncovered, for 3–4 days. This starts the skin drying out and facilitates good crackling.*

SERVES 6

PRAWNS FLAMBÉED WITH AGED CARIBBEAN RUM SERVED WITH FRIED PLANTAINS & SPICY GREEN TOMATO SAUCE

The inspiration for this dish comes from time spent at Blue Heaven restaurant in the Florida Keys with my friend Dan Hatch, who specialises in Caribbean cooking. The green tomato salsa that I really enjoyed using there was not readily available here in New Zealand, so we sourced a really good one in Italy which I now cannot be without. It is a winner with cold meats and cheese as well as how it is utilised in this recipe. And though it can be omitted, don't do so lightly — it adds a important dimension to the dish.

1 plantain or a long, thin kumara
1 litre canola oil
1 tsp flaky salt

plantain (optional)

Using a mandolin or potato peeler, slice the unpeeled plantain or kumara lengthways into thin, 1mm strips. Heat the oil in a saucepan to 175°C, then place the plantain strips into the oil and cook until they turn golden brown (approximately 1–2 minutes). Remove from the oil and place onto paper towels, then sprinkle with the flaky salt. When cool, store in an airtight container until needed.

36 whole medium-sized black tiger prawns
flaky salt
100ml Pukara extra-virgin olive oil
180ml Caribbean dark rum

prawns

Remove the heads from the prawns and place them belly-side down on a chopping board. Make an incision along the back through the shell and flesh, but stop short of cutting through the belly shell and therefore splitting them in half. Flatten them, then lightly bruise the flesh with the back of a knife. Season with the flaky salt. Heat the oil to a shimmer in a large sauté pan. Cook the prawns in the pan, belly-side down. Once the shells have turned completely orange, turn the prawns over and cook for another minute. Add the rum, then flame to burn off the alcohol and toss the prawns through the residual liquid. Remove the pan from the heat, leaving the prawns in the pan, and set aside briefly. Prawns are done once the flesh turns pink and the heat of the rest of the dish will finish cooking them.

2 tbsp canola oil
120g shallots, *finely diced*
3 tsp finely grated fresh ginger
600ml fish stock *(see page 231)*
1 lemon, *cut into 6 wedges*
5 tbsp Worcestershire sauce
3 tbsp fresh lime juice
2 tsp Tabasco garlic pepper sauce
75g unsalted butter
120g tomato concasse *(see page 233)*
6 tbsp chopped coriander leaves
9 tbsp green tomato salsa *(see page 239 Salsa di Pomodori Verdi)*

sauce

In a sauté pan, heat the oil to a shimmer. Cook the shallots and ginger over a medium heat until the shallots are translucent. Add the fish stock, lemon wedges, Worcestershire sauce, lime juice and Tabasco sauce. Reduce by half over a moderate heat. While the sauce is simmering, whisk in the butter so that it is absorbed (this will also help to thicken the sauce). Add the tomato concasse, coriander and green tomato salsa and stir through. Pour the sauce over the prawns in the other pan.

assembly

Arrange the prawns in neat piles on six heated plates, then pour any remaining sauce over them. Garnish with the plantain chips.

SIMON SAYS *Cooking prawns in the shell makes the flesh taste sweeter. If frozen, it is best to thaw the prawns in the refrigerator, but if they must be thawed in a hurry leave them in the sealed pack and thaw them under cold running water. Never thaw in the sink at room temperature or by using hot water.*

SERVES 6

ALASKAN KING CRAB RISOTTO WITH WASABI TOBIKO CAVIAR

More years ago than I care to remember, I dined with a great chef friend of mine, Jason McDonald, in his New Orleans restaurant where he introduced me to tobiko, the Japanese name for flying fish roe. The roe or eggs are small, from 0.5mm–0.8mm. Plain tobiko has a red-orange color, a mild smoky/salty taste and a crunchy texture. The roe is coloured with wasabi (green), ginger (pale orange) or squid ink (black). The flavours, colours and texture make this one of the most interesting garnishes available. Processed in Japan, it was the very first product I imported into New Zealand. Shipped frozen, it lasts for months in the freezer and even in its frozen state can be easily separated, making it practical to use in small amounts.

1.2 litres fish, crab or vegetable stock
3 tbsp basmati rice
50g salted butter
3 tbsp Pukara extra-virgin olive oil
4 medium shallots, *finely diced*
2 medium cloves garlic, *minced*
1½ cups Arborio rice
200ml white wine
700g Alaskan red king crab meat, *removed from the shell and diced*
50g Parmigiano-Reggiano, *grated*
30 rocket leaves, *finely chopped*
dash of Tabasco green pepper sauce *(jalapeño)*
cracked black pepper
salt, *preferably Italian herb salt*

risotto

In a saucepan, bring the stock, basmati rice and half the butter to the boil (while the stock itself will be used in the risotto, the basmati rice will be discarded — see note below). In another saucepan, heat the olive oil to a shimmer. Add the shallots and garlic and sauté until translucent, then add the Arborio rice and sauté for 3 minutes, stirring continuously with a wooden spoon. Add the wine and stir over a low–medium heat until the rice absorbs the wine. Stir in half a cup of the hot stock, avoiding the basmati rice in the pan. Continue stirring to ensure the Arborio rice does not catch. When the liquid has been absorbed, add another half a cup at a time until all the stock has been absorbed. This process should take 25–30 minutes and the rice should be al dente. Add the crab meat, grated cheese, remaining butter and the rocket. Season with a dash of Tabasco sauce and some cracked black pepper and salt (a word of caution: go easy on the salt because the Tabasco is salty).

6 crab claws
6 tbsp wasabi tobiko caviar
1 lemon, *cut into 6 wedges*

assembly

Heat the crab claws in a steamer, oven or microwave. Divide the risotto between the plates and garnish each with 1 tablespoon of wasabi tobiko caviar, a crab claw and a wedge of lemon.

SIMON SAYS *Adding the basmati rice to the stock gives the risotto a creamier texture; this is due to the starchiness in the basmati rice being released while cooking in the liquid. Note that the basmati is discarded after making the simple stock. I picked up this invaluable trick while working with a talented young Italian chef on the island of Pantelleria, off Sicily.*

SERVES 6

STEAMED ALASKAN RED KING CRAB WITH A TRIO OF SMOKED CHIPOTLE, GINGER & GARLIC BUTTERS

My first encounter with Smoky Tabasco Chipotle pepper sauce was in Reno, Nevada — I try to travel there each year to extend my culinary knowledge. Quite coincidentally, I found that the Reno Air Races always take place at the very same time I'm there; it is a source of ongoing wonderment to me. While in Reno I always meet up with Tom Taylor, who I like to think of as a friend. A NASA hypersonic genius, he knows a good deal about rockets and rocket fuel, which brings me to the Tabasco. Well, in truth it really isn't that hot, but its smoky flavour makes it an absolute winner for so many spicy dishes and it is just spectacular with this Alaskan king crab.

smoked chipotle butter
250g unsalted clarified butter
50ml Tabasco chipotle pepper sauce
   (smoked)
1 tsp salt

garlic butter
250g unsalted clarified butter
45g minced garlic
1½ tsp salt

ginger butter
250g unsalted clarified butter
60g grated fresh ginger
1½ tsp salt

100g butter
2.4kg large Alaskan red king crab legs

3 lemons

special equipment *steamer (optional)*

flavoured butters
Heat each measure of clarified butter in three separate saucepans until it melts. To the first saucepan, add the smoked chipotle Tabasco sauce and the salt. To the second saucepan, add the minced garlic and salt; and to the third, add the ginger and salt. Set aside the three saucepans to keep warm for 30 minutes so the flavourings have time to infuse. Pour the flavoured butters into separate warm dishes ready for serving (ramekins are best).

crab
Melt the butter so it will be ready to brush onto the heated crab legs. There are several ways to heat crab, the best being in a steamer. Place the crab into the steamer and steam for 5 minutes. If you do not have a steamer, in the oven or on the barbecue for a short time are acceptable alternatives. Using a pastry brush, brush the crab legs liberally with the melted butter.

assembly
Cut the lemons in half, then cut each half into three. Remove the seeds and reserve the wedges in the refrigerator ready for use. Serve the crab with the warm flavoured butters and the lemon wedges.

SERVES 6

AKAROA SALMON ON A DUET OF BARLEY & LENTILS WITH CORIANDER YOGHURT

I have used Akaroa Salmon for some years now and will go out on a limb and state categorically that there is no finer salmon available in New Zealand. In 1984 Tom Bates, an Akaroa farmer, set up a salmon farm in Lucas Bay. The bay is near the Akaroa Harbour entrance, ensuring good current flow; it is also sheltered and offers deep water close in to the rocky coast. Akaroa Salmon grows, processes, packs and markets their salmon in such a way that I am able to present it in the restaurant within 24 hours of it leaving the water. Akaroa Salmon is totally owned by the Bates family i.e. 100% New Zealand owned — a testament to the determination of Tom Bates.

75g pearl barley
900ml vegetable stock
75g puy lentils
50ml Pukara extra-virgin olive oil
180g shallots, *finely diced*
½ medium carrot, *finely diced*
1 tsp grated fresh ginger
½ stick celery, *finely diced*
300ml Madeira jus *(see page 232)*
450g tomato concasse *(see page 233)*
40g unsalted butter
6 tbsp chopped coriander
1 tsp cracked black pepper
1 tsp flaky salt
100ml vegetable stock, *extra*

450g plain unsweetened yoghurt
9 tbsp chopped coriander
2 tbsp fresh lime juice

6 x 200g portions Akaroa Salmon, *skin on, boned*
1 tsp flaky salt
¼ tsp ground white pepper
50ml Pukara extra-virgin olive oil

barley & lentils
Soak the barley overnight in cold water. Divide the stock evenly between two separate saucepans and place the lentils in one and the barley in the other. Allow the lentils to simmer for 12–15 minutes; the barley will take about 20–25 minutes on a slightly higher heat. Once cooked, strain them and mix them together before setting aside briefly.

In a saucepan, heat the oil to a shimmer. Add the shallots, carrot, ginger and celery and cook without colouring any of the vegetables for 4 minutes over a medium–high heat. Add the lentils and barley, Madeira jus and tomato concasse and bring to a gentle simmer. Whisk in the butter until it is all absorbed then add the coriander, pepper and salt. Use the additional vegetable stock to adjust the consistency of the barley and lentil mix only if it is too dry.

coriander yoghurt
In a bowl, mix together the yoghurt, coriander and lime juice.

salmon
Dry the skin-side of the salmon with paper towels. Score the salmon skin lengthways with the tip of a sharp knife, just piercing the skin. Season the salmon with the salt and pepper. Heat the oil to a shimmer in a sauté pan. Carefully place the salmon skin-side down into the pan and allow the skin to crisp for 3–4 minutes, then turn the fish over, lower the heat and cook the other side for 2–3 minutes. Remove from the pan and set on paper towels to absorb any excess oil.

assembly
Divide the lentils between six heated plates. Place the cooked salmon on top of the lentils, then dress with the coriander yoghurt.

SIMON SAYS *Testing fish for doneness is really quite easy — prise the flesh apart with a fork and look inside. Remember that the fish will continue to cook after it is removed from the heat, so remove it before it is ready for plating. Most fish taste best when they flake and are opaque. Salmon and trout are the exception to the rule, in that they taste better on the rare side, when the centre is still translucent.*

SERVES 6

SEAFOOD RISOTTO WITH SCALLOPS, PRAWNS & CALAMARI TOPPED WITH FLOUNDER CRACKLING & TEMPURA ANCHOVY

Flounder frames, a term perhaps not so familiar to many, are the skeletal remains of filleted flounders. Fried until they are crispy, they can be used as a garnish in the same way one would use pork crackling.

flounder crackling

500ml canola oil
6 flounder frames, *head removed*
6 tbsp cornflour
1 tsp sea salt
1 tsp cracked black pepper

In a high-sided 25–30cm saucepan heat the canola oil to 150°C (take care because hot oil is potentially very dangerous). Alternatively, a deep fryer is a good option. Scrape any residual flesh from the flounder frames. Using a pair of scissors, trim off the pointy fins from along the sides and discard. Place the cornflour and salt and pepper in a shallow bowl and mix well. Dust each flounder frame with the seasoned cornflour and shake off any excess. Carefully lower each of the floured frames into the hot oil, one at time, turning every 30 seconds so that it cooks evenly, for about 6–8 minutes and it turns golden brown. Drain on paper towels set over a rolling pin, using tongs to hold the frame in a curved shape until it cools and sets hard. Keep in a warm place. Retain the oil for later use.

risotto

1 litre fish, crab, clam or vegetable stock
3 tbsp basmati rice
50g butter
3 tbsp Pukara extra-virgin olive oil
4 medium shallots, *finely diced*
2 medium cloves garlic, *minced*
1½ cups Arborio rice
200ml white wine
2 tbsp Pukara extra-virgin olive oil
3 calamari tubes
500g fresh scallops
500g prawn cutlets
50g smoked provolone, *finely chopped*
1 tbsp finely chopped chives
1 tsp ground black pepper
2 tbsp butter

In a saucepan, bring the stock, basmati rice and the butter to the boil. Let it stand off the heat for 5 minutes. Strain through a fine sieve and retain the stock, discarding the rice. In a saucepan, heat the first measure of olive oil to a shimmer. Add the shallots and garlic and sauté until soft. Add the Arborio rice and sauté for 3 minutes, stirring continuously with a wooden spoon. Add the wine and stir over a moderate heat until the rice absorbs the wine. Stir in half a cup of hot rice stock, stirring continuously to ensure the Arborio rice does not catch. When it has been absorbed, continue adding the stock half a cup at a time until all the stock has been absorbed. This process should take 25–30 minutes and the rice should be al dente. While the risotto is cooking, heat the second measure of olive oil to a shimmer in a frying pan and quickly sauté the calamari, scallops and prawns for 2 minutes. Once the risotto has taken in all the stock, add the sautéed seafood, provolone, chives, black pepper and the second measure of butter. Fold through carefully and place back on the heat, covered, for 2 minutes to warm through.

tempura anchovy

6 good-quality anchovy fillets
12 large fresh sage leaves
3 tbsp plain flour
250ml tempura batter *(see page 233)*

Individually sandwich the 6 anchovy fillets between pairs of sage leaves, leaf rib side in. Press together to seal and dust with plain flour. Reheat the retained oil and slip the sandwiches into the pre-prepared tempura batter, run off the excess batter and cook in the oil for 1 minute on each side. Drain on a paper towel and keep warm with the flounder crackling.

assembly

salt
2 tbsp lemon oil *(optional)*

Place a warm flounder crackling on each of six serving plates, season with salt then divide the risotto among the crackling, ensuring that each serving has an even mix of seafood. Arrange a tempura anchovy on top and, if desired, drizzle a little lemon oil around the plate.

SERVES 6

TOASTED CRAYFISH SANDWICH WITH PROVOLONE & MOZZARELLA

This would have to win the nomination for the most decadent sandwich since sliced bread. I guess its origins lie with those lucky souls who had the ability and opportunity to catch their own sandwich filling. It would be a trifle more difficult to catch the source of the mozzarella garnish. If you are acquainted with the massive Italian water buffalo, you will understand where I am coming from — or going to, if the beast happens to be indulging in a bit of free ranging.

3 x 600g live crayfish *(lobster)*
1 large bowl iced water

crayfish

The crayfish should be cooked one at a time so that the temperature of the water is maintained. Bring 6 litres of water to the boil in an 11 litre saucepan. Carefully place the crayfish into the pan. Cook for 6 minutes, then remove the crayfish and refresh in the iced water immediately. Once the crayfish has cooled, wrap a tea towel around the body. Holding the body firmly, remove the tail. Place the tail on a chopping board and slit it lengthways down the middle. Open it out, and carefully remove the flesh and slice it into 5mm thick pieces. Set aside until needed. Alaskan king crab leg meat can be substituted for the crayfish and — unless the crayfish supply is bountiful and free — is probably a less expensive option.

12 slices white toast bread
60g butter, *softened*
180g provolone, *grated*
6 small vine-ripened tomatoes, *sliced*
6 tbsp chopped chives
540g cooked crayfish meat *(see Simon Says)*
½ tsp ground white pepper
2 x 125g balls buffalo mozzarella, *sliced*

sandwich

Butter the bread on one side only. Lay out six slices, buttered-side down, and arrange the following ingredients in this order on each slice: one-sixth of the provolone, 1 sliced tomato, 1 tablespoon chopped chives, one-sixth of the crayfish, white pepper and one-sixth of the sliced mozzarella. Top each pile of ingredients with one of the remaining bread slices, buttered-side up. Toast the sandwiches, one or two at a time, in the sandwich toaster or panini machine, on a medium setting for approximately 5–8 minutes. Once cooked, remove from the sandwich maker and leave to sit for 1–2 minutes. Using a serrated knife, cut off the crusts, then cut each sandwich into two triangles.

2 tbsp orange balsamic mousse *(see page 235)*
100g fresh rocket
1 tbsp Pukara extra-virgin olive oil
3 x 125g balls buffalo mozzarella
18 small vine-ripened tomatoes, *still on the vine*

special equipment *panini machine or toasted sandwich maker*

assembly

Spoon 1 teaspoon of orange balsamic mousse on each plate to make a squiggly shape, then position two sandwich triangles next to it. Mix together the rocket and oil, then transfer a portion onto the plate next to the sandwich. Alongside place half a mozzarella ball and three tomatoes, still attached to their vine.

SIMON SAYS *A 600g crayfish will yield around 180g of flesh.*
For presentation purposes the sandwich should be allowed to rest for 1–2 minutes before cutting so that the cheese will not be forced out.

SERVES 6

simon's favourites

CAESAR SALAD RISOTTO WITH SLOW-POACHED EGG, MALPIGHI BALSAMIC & SAGE AND ANCHOVY CHIPS

Risotto is one of the most common ways of cooking rice in Italy. Properly cooked, it is rich and creamy but the grains remain separate and al dente. This recipe is far from a traditional risotto, but it has all the basic elements, with elaborations based on the traditional Caesar salad.

bacon

6 rashers streaky bacon

Preheat the oven to 180°C. Line a baking tray with baking paper, arrange the bacon on the tray and cook for 4–6 minutes or until the bacon is crispy. Pat dry on paper towels, chop roughly and set aside.

sage and anchovy chips

6 anchovy fillets, *ideally same length as the sage leaves*
12 fresh sage leaves, *all roughly the same size*
150ml olive oil
2 tbsp plain flour
100ml tempura batter *(see page 233)*

On absorbent paper towels, pat the oil from the anchovies. Arrange the sage leaves in pairs of roughly matching size. Place six leaves onto a chopping board with the upper side of the leaf to the board. Place an anchovy fillet on each and press down gently with a matching leaf to make a sage and anchovy sandwich. Heat the olive oil to 160°C. Dredge the sage sandwiches in flour then dip into the tempura batter and fry until crispy; remove and drain on paper towels.

slow-poached eggs

6 free-range eggs

About 15 minutes prior to starting the risotto, bring a large saucepan of water to 65°C (regulate with a thermometer). Gently place the whole eggs in the water and cook for 45 minutes. Remove the eggs and place in an egg carton (to facilitate removal of the top of the shell later).

risotto

1100ml chicken or vegetable stock
4 tbsp Pukara extra-virgin olive oil
2 tbsp unsalted butter
1 medium white onion, *finely diced*
1 clove garlic, *finely diced*
400g Arborio rice
150ml dry white wine
1 tsp Murray River salt
60g Parmigiano-Reggiano, *grated*
1 cup roughly chopped baby cos lettuce leaves
160ml Caesar aïoli *(see page 38)*

Heat the stock. In a separate saucepan, heat the olive oil and half the butter. Add the onion and garlic and sauté very slowly for 5–6 minutes, until the onion is translucent. Add the rice and increase the heat, stirring constantly to coat the rice with the oil and butter so that it takes on a glossy appearance and becomes slightly translucent. Add the white wine. Once this has been absorbed, add the salt. Gradually start adding the hot stock, one ladleful at a time, ensuring the heat is not too high; a medium simmer is best so the rice doesn't cook too quickly. This process should take 25–30 minutes. When all the stock has been absorbed, fold in the cooked bacon, sprinkle over the grated Parmigiano-Reggiano and top with the remaining butter. Cover and allow to sit for 5 minutes. Just before serving, use a wooden spoon to fold through half the chopped cos lettuce and Caesar dressing.

assembly

40g Parmigiano-Reggiano, *shaved*
salt
cracked black pepper
4 tsp Malpighi aged balsamic vinegar, *12 years old or more*

Carefully remove the top part of the shell from each egg. Divide the risotto between the bowls and, using the base of the egg shell, create an indentation in the middle of each risotto serving. Gently pour the warmed egg into the indented risotto. Grind a little black pepper onto each egg and garnish with the remaining baby cos lettuce leaves, shaved Parmigiano-Reggiano, and sage and anchovy chips. Drizzle aged Malpighi balsamic on each serving at the table.

SERVES 6

SLOW-POACHED EGG ON SOFT MUSHROOM POLENTA WITH SHAVED TRUFFLE

When describing this dish to a table of guests, I often substitute the word porridge for polenta; it tends to focus the mind and certainly gains me undivided attention. Reactions vary from undisguised concern for my mental state to open scepticism. However, reservations are largely dispelled when the dish is served and then evaporate entirely as it is consumed. I believe that thinking and dining outside the square is great fun and we need to do more of it. My father still recalls a meal in Italy that involved being served a final course (after the dessert) of fried eggs with fresh truffle shaved over them. Fabulous!

slow-poached eggs

6 free-range eggs

Bring a large saucepan of water to 65°C (regulate with a thermometer). Gently place the whole eggs in the water and cook for 45 minutes. Remove the eggs and stand them in an egg carton (this will facilitate removal of the top of the shell later).

polenta

1 litre vegetable stock
500ml milk
100ml cream
150g instant polenta
2 tbsp mascarpone
3 tbsp finely grated Parmigiano-Reggiano
70g cooked porcini *(see page 238)* or field mushrooms
120g porcini paste *(see page 239 Crema di Funghi Porcini)*
2 tsp salt
¼ tsp ground black pepper

Begin this 35 minutes into the egg-cooking time. In a medium–large saucepan, bring the stock, milk and cream to the boil, then slowly whisk in the polenta. Turn the heat down to medium and continue stirring with a wooden spoon for 3 minutes until the mixture thickens. Remove the mixture from the heat and allow to cool slightly. Add the mascarpone, Parmigiano-Reggiano, porcini mushrooms and porcini paste. Season with salt and pepper.

assembly

salt
cracked black pepper
1 whole truffle *(see page 238) (optional)*
3 tsp white truffle oil

Carefully remove the top part of the shell from each egg. Divide the polenta between six serving bowls. Using one of the eggs or the back of a spoon, create a depression in the middle of each serving of polenta. Pour a warmed egg into each indentation. Season the egg with salt and cracked black pepper. Garnish with a little sliced truffle and drizzle half a teaspoon of truffle oil over each serving.

SERVES 6

ROCKET REFRESHER

This can be served between courses instead of a sorbet. As the recipe makes 1 litre, halving the ingredients would allow smaller glasses to be used if preferred. It should be served immediately because the ingredients will separate if left to stand.

small bunch of rocket (*arugula*)
250g peeled and deseeded rock melon
1 cup gingerale
100g ice
1½ cups yoghurt sorbet (*see page 234*)
40 mint leaves
2 limes, *peeled*

Blend all the ingredients for 1 minute or until well blended. Pour into six tall champagne flutes.

SERVES 6

CANDIED PECAN KUMARA

This recipe originated in New Orleans and is very sweet and rich as the ingredients suggest. The pecans are particularly nice both in texture and as a foil to the sweetness. This is a very popular side dish with those who enjoy something a little sweet.

75g butter
100g brown sugar
100ml cream
2 tbsp dark rum, *preferably Appletons or Mt Gay*

2kg orange kumara
50g butter
2 tsp salt
1 tsp white pepper

200ml cream
18 whole pecans, *split in half*

caramel sauce

In a saucepan over a medium heat, melt the butter and sugar, then add the cream and bring to the boil. Add the rum and simmer for 2 minutes. Allow to cool.

kumara

Preheat the oven to 160°C. Roast the whole kumara for 1½ hours or until soft in the middle. Allow to cool. Peel the kumara, then place them in a colander for 5–10 minutes to allow any liquid to drain out of them. Transfer the kumara to a food processor and add ½ cup of the caramel sauce, the butter, salt and white pepper. Process until it reaches purée consistency.

assembly

Preheat the oven to 180°C. Divide the kumara mix into six ovenproof side dishes. Mix the remaining caramel sauce with the cream and pour around the kumara. Push three pecans out of sight into each serving and place another three on top, then heat the dishes in the oven until the cream begins to bubble and the kumara is hot in the middle.

SERVES 6

BEEF CHEEK & PEPPER STEW IN PÈPPOLI WINE SAUCE

The Chianti Classico I have chosen for this dish hails from the Pèppoli estate, one of the Antinori vineyards in Tuscany. Antinori has been in the wine-making business for 26 generations, going as far back as 1385, so I figure they have got the knack of it by now. Made with predominantly sangiovese grapes with merlot and syrah in the minority, it is very fruity — even at a young age — and I find it ideally suited to this dish.

2kg beef cheeks
3 large carrots, *roughly diced*
2 medium-sized onions, *roughly diced*
4 large stalks celery, *roughly diced*
1 bottle Antinori Pèppoli Chianti Classico
30g black peppercorns
8 sprigs of thyme
2 sprigs of rosemary
2 tsp salt
100g plain flour
4 tbsp Pukara extra-virgin olive oil
3 cloves garlic, *crushed*
4 bay leaves
6 green olives, *roughly chopped*
3 litres beef stock

beef cheeks

Trim the beef cheeks of any fat and obvious sinew. Place the carrots, onion and celery in a large saucepan or bowl. Place the beef cheeks on top, then pour the wine over the contents so the cheeks are submerged. Add the peppercorns, thyme and rosemary. Cover and leave to marinate overnight.

Preheat the oven to 200°C. Remove the beef cheeks from the marinade and pat dry with a clean cloth or paper towels. Strain the wine into a clean saucepan and place over a medium–high heat and reduce by half. Reserve the marinated vegetables and herbs for later use. Season the meat with salt, dredge in the flour and pat off the excess. Heat the oil until shimmering in a sauté pan. Add the meat and sear on all sides until brown. Transfer to a casserole dish along with the reserved vegetables and herbs. Add the garlic, reduced wine, bay leaves, olives and stock. Cover and cook in the oven for 2½–3 hours, checking and maintaining the fluid level throughout (test for tenderness and moistness after 2½ hours). When the meat is ready, remove from the cooking liquor and set aside, covered. Pour the liquor into a saucepan, bring to the boil and reduce until it is of sauce consistency. Strain and taste, adjusting the seasoning to your personal preference.

black pepper
6 sprigs of thyme

assembly

Reheat the beef cheeks in the sauce. Divide the meat between six heated plates. Spoon the sauce over each portion and serve with an extra grind of black pepper. Garnish each with a sprig of fresh thyme.

SERVES 6

SQUAB BREAST ON CIABATTA LOADED WITH MUSHROOM & FOIE GRAS GREEN PEPPERCORN SAUCE

While many people shy away from squab (young pigeon), it remains one of my favourite dishes. If you are unsure how your guests feel about it, tell them that what they are enjoying is Argentinian beef. Once established that it tastes great, the truth can be revealed. On the other hand, if you don't lie particularly convincingly, or are catering for truly conservative diners, then perhaps it's best to substitute chicken for the squab.

3 squab, *each weighing 350g*

squab

Remove the breast meat from each squab, reserving the carcasses for the sauce. Remove the skin from the breasts and discard.

45ml Pukara extra-virgin olive oil
1 large carrot, *roughly chopped*
1 medium white onion, *roughly chopped*
3 medium cloves garlic, *crushed*
2 large stalks celery, *roughly chopped*
3 litres water
250ml cabernet merlot
6 whole green peppercorns
3 bay leaves
1 sprig of thyme
6 sage leaves
1 cup port
8 whole green peppercorns, *finely ground*
6g porcini stock powder *(or mushroom stock powder)*
30ml brandy
140g cooked porcini mushrooms
70g porcini paste *(see page 239 Crema di Funghi Porcini)*

sauce

In a large saucepan over a medium heat, bring the olive oil to a shimmer. Sauté the carrot, onion, garlic and celery for 5 minutes, stirring with a wooden spoon. Add the squab carcasses followed by the water, wine, peppercorns, bay leaves, thyme and sage leaves. Bring to the boil, then reduce to a simmer for 2 hours, skimming off and discarding any scum that rises to the surface. Strain and discard all the solid items; this should leave approximately 1 litre of stock. Return the strained stock to a clean saucepan and bring back to a simmer. Add the port, the ground green peppercorns and the stock powder. Reduce by three-quarters so that you have just 250ml of concentrated sauce. Add the brandy, cooked porcini and porcini paste and bring to the boil for 1 minute. Set aside until required.

100ml canola oil
6 sage leaves

sage chips

In a high-sided 25–30cm saucepan, heat the canola oil to 150°C (or set a deep fryer to this temperature). Take great care with the hot oil as it is potentially very dangerous. Carefully place the sage leaves in the oil and remove after 30 seconds or when they become crispy, but before they change colour. Drain on paper towels and set aside until required.

6 slices ciabatta *(approximately half a loaf)*
30ml Pukara extra-virgin olive oil
salt and pepper
40g foie gras
1 clove garlic, *halved*

assembly

Preheat the oven to 180°C. Brush both sides of the ciabatta with the olive oil. Season the squab breasts on both sides. Heat the olive oil to a shimmer, then sauté the squab breasts for 30 seconds on each side. Place on a tray in the oven with the ciabatta for 5 minutes. Remove the squab from the oven and allow them to rest on a chopping board for 6 minutes. Reheat the sauce and stir in the foie gras. Remove the ciabatta from the oven and rub each slice with the cut side of the garlic clove. Arrange two slices on each serving plate. Cut each squab breast in half and place a piece on each ciabatta slice. Pour over some sauce, then arrange a second piece of squab on top. Garnish with a sage chip.

SERVES 6

JERVOIS STEAK HOUSE PRIME RIB WITH HORSERADISH & PARSLEY OIL

Years ago, when my dad was flying internationally, I periodically went away with him and we always had a prime rib meal during a stay in Honolulu. The beef was so unbelievably tender I just had to find out how they managed it. I worked hard on establishing a relationship with the chef, trying to get him to tell me how he prepared and cooked it. Initially I had as much success as a politician trying to give a straight answer. Eventually, however — I think more to get rid of me than anything else — the chef took me through the process. But now, because the beef we use in our restaurants has better flavour, I believe that what we serve surpasses the beef that so impressed me initially. Red meat — and by that I don't mean rare-cooked meat — comes in for a good deal of criticism, but in my view, if eaten as part of a properly balanced diet, the odd lump of 'bull's bum' isn't going to do a body any harm at all.

SIMON SAYS *Ensure the butcher removes the chine bone: the spine to which the ribs are joined. If this is not done, the ribs will be very difficult to separate when it comes time to serve them. We use Australian Black Angus beef aged 36 months that has been fed for the final 150 days on grain. The rib is larger than we are able to procure locally and the flavour is exceptionally good, which can in part be attributed to the feeding regime, and the meat itself is very tender, reflecting well on the care of the animals both prior to and after slaughter. We age our beef for at least eight weeks in very carefully controlled conditions at a temperature of just 1°C.*

Purchase the largest four-rib piece available. Be sure to buy it from a dedicated butcher and not from some anonymous source where you are unable to personally discuss the merits of your selection with a knowledgeable butcher.

prime rib

3 tbsp Pukara extra-virgin olive oil
2 tbsp salt
1 tbsp cracked black pepper
4 x prime rib roasts *(3–3.5kg)*

Preheat the oven to 220°C. In a small bowl, mix together the olive oil and salt and pepper. Using a sharp knife, slice under the fat of the meat until it is possible to lift three-quarters of it away from the roast, but don't remove it. With a pastry brush, paint the entire prime rib with the olive oil seasoning, including under the flap of fat, then fold the flap back over the roast. Place the meat in a roasting dish bone-side down and cook for 20 minutes. Reduce the heat to 160°C and continue cooking until the internal temperature reaches 48°C (about 1 hour 15 minutes–1 hour 30 minutes). Begin checking the internal temperature 20 minutes before the calculated end of the cooking time; there is no way back if the meat is overcooked. Ensure that the thermometer is inserted into the thickest part of the meat, not touching the fat or bone. When the internal temperature of 48°C is reached, remove the meat from the oven, cover with tin foil and allow it to rest for 30 minutes before carving. The internal temperature of the meat will continue to rise by about another 10 degrees which will bring the roast to the desired temperature of 58°C.

parsley oil

60g curly parsley
135ml Pukara extra-virgin olive oil

Separate the curly parsley leaves from the stalks and place in a bowl. Pour boiling water over and stir for 30 seconds. Drain off the hot water and transfer the parsley to a bowl of ice-cold water to cool. Drain the parsley, then wring it dry using a clean tea towel. Place the dried parsley in a blender and blend with the olive oil for 3 minutes. Remove the

resulting purée and strain through a muslin cloth or fat filter, making sure to squeeze all the oil out of the filter. Use rubber gloves to avoid staining your hands. Transfer the oil to a small squeeze bottle ready to garnish the plate. This recipe makes more than is needed but it will keep well in the refrigerator for four days.

6 tbsp horseradish sauce (preferably Royalty brand)
rosemary and garlic-flavoured balsamic mousse

special equipment meat thermometer

assembly
Slice the meat to the desired thickness or remove all the bones for ease of slicing. Drizzle some squiggles of balsamic mousse on each plate, then squeeze some parsley oil, through the middle to make an attractive garnish. Serve the meat with a tablespoon of horseradish sauce.

SIMON SAYS *Remove the roast from the refrigerator 2 hours before cooking to allow it to reach room temperature, which means easier cooking with less drying out of the outer layer. It is always best to cook meat on the bone; it facilitates the even transference of heat during cooking and improves the flavour.*

Balsamic mousses of varying flavours are available from good delicatessens. They are, as the name suggests, thicker then balsamic vinegar and hold their shape so are ideal for decorative effects that also have a distinctive flavour.

SERVES 6

CHICKEN LIVER PÂTÉ & BEEF CHEEK IN BRIOCHE

When we introduced this dish at Shed 5 restaurant, it was a great success from day one. As an entrée it falls into the rich category, but it has the contrasting textures of beef cheek and pâté along with the rich sauce that infiltrates the brioche to make it quite different. The room-temperature chicken liver paté makes a delightful contrast to the hot beef and rich sauce.

chicken liver pâté

200g chicken livers
150ml port
100ml Marsala
30ml olive oil
75g shallots
4 sprigs of thyme, *stalks discarded*
1 sprig of marjoram, *stalk discarded*
1½ tsp flaky salt
2 eggs
200g butter, *melted*

Trim the livers of any fat, then marinate them for 2 hours in the port and Marsala. Remove the livers from the marinade and set aside. Heat the wine mixture in a saucepan over a high heat to reduce by half. Set aside. In another saucepan, heat the olive oil to a shimmer and sauté the shallots with the thyme and marjoram until the shallots are translucent. Transfer to a food processor and add the livers along with the salt, reduced wines and eggs, one at a time. Once the eggs have been processed, blend in the butter. Pass the mixture through a fine sieve. Preheat the oven to 100°C. Pour the liver mixture into a terrine mould or a loaf tin lined with cling film, tap the container on the bench to remove any air bubbles, then cover with tin foil. Place into a deep baking dish lined with a tea towel. Pour enough hot water into the tray to come halfway up the side of the mould. Bake for approximately 1 hour 15 minutes or until the chicken liver mixture is set all the way through. A skewer inserted into the middle should be clean when removed. (Note: the centre should still be quite pink.) Chill overnight.

beef cheeks

500g beef cheek
1 large carrot, *roughly diced*
1 medium-sized onion, *roughly diced*
1 large stalk celery, *roughly diced*
375ml chianti
10 black peppercorns
1 large sprig of rosemary, *5cm long*
5 large sprigs of thyme, *5cm long*
¼ teaspoons salt
1 tbsp plain flour
2 tbsp Pukara extra-virgin olive oil
2 cloves garlic
2 bay leaves
4 green olives, *pitted and chopped*
800ml beef stock

Trim the beef cheeks of any fat and obvious sinew. Place the carrot, onion and celery in a large saucepan or bowl. Place the beef cheeks on top, then pour the chianti over the contents so the cheeks are submerged. Add the peppercorns, rosemary and thyme. Cover and leave to marinate overnight.

Preheat the oven to 200°C. Remove the beef cheeks from the marinade and pat dry with a clean cloth or paper towels. Strain the wine into a clean saucepan, place over a medium–high heat and reduce by half. Reserve the marinated vegetables and herbs for later use. Season the meat with salt, dredge in the flour and pat off the excess. Heat the oil until shimmering in a sauté pan. Add the meat and sear on all sides until brown. Transfer to a casserole dish along with the reserved vegetables and herbs. Add the garlic, reduced wine, bay leaves, chopped olives and stock. Cover and cook in the oven for 2½–3 hours, checking and maintaining the fluid level throughout (test for tenderness and moistness after 2½ hours). When the meat is ready, remove from the cooking liquor and set aside, covered. Pour the cooking liquor into a saucepan, bring to the boil and reduce until it is of sauce consistency. Strain and taste, adjusting the seasoning to taste.

brioche

6 muffin-sized brioche buns *(see page 230)*

Cut a 1cm slice from the top of each brioche bun (reserve to use for mopping up sauce). Using a small serrated knife, carefully scoop out the centre of the bun so that only the outer crust is left as a shell.

300ml canola oil
18 sage leaves

assembly
Preheat the oven to 180°C. Remove the pâté from the refrigerator and allow it to reach room temperature. In a saucepan heat the oil to 165°C. Using paper towels, pat dry the sage leaves, then deep fry them for a few seconds in the oil until the leaves have a wet look about them. Remove from the oil and place on a paper towel.

Cut the beef cheek into 5mm thick slices, allowing five slices per portion. Heat the sliced meat in the oven at the same time as the brioche shells, until the latter are hot and crispy. Place a brioche bun onto each warmed plate, then arrange five slices of beef cheek in the cavity with enough of the cheek exposed for presentation. Place an oval-shaped scoop of pâté into the cavity beside the beef cheek with half of it exposed. Pour enough of the hot sauce over the sliced cheek so it fills the brioche bun and overflows onto the plate. Finish by placing a crispy fried sage leaf on top.

SIMON SAYS *When purchasing livers, look for those that are pale yellowish in colour; they will be fatter, sweeter and less bitter than the dark red ones. Frozen livers should be defrosted in the refrigerator so they don't lose too much moisture. Discard the liquid that collects during defrosting, along with any discolored pieces of liver. For best results, soak the livers in milk overnight.*

SERVES 6

SHED 5 WHOLE ROASTED FISH WITH SHELLFISH & SPICY TOMATO FUMET

This menu item is a long-time favourite at our Shed 5 restaurant, where we have a dedicated fish filleting room and can really do justice to the unique delicacy of New Zealand seafood. Littleneck hard-shell clams, or cockles as we call them, are a delicacy, but their sweet taste and delicate texture are often forgotten when they are improperly prepared and sand is unpleasantly present. If you can enjoy the luxury of collecting the cockles yourself, leave them immersed in a bucket of clean sea water for 12 hours to allow the shellfish to expel all the sand. An acceptable and equally successful alternative is to add one-third of a cup of salt to each 4.5 litres of fresh soaking water. Use a large amount of water or change it frequently to prevent suffocating the shellfish through oxygen depletion.

2 x 600g whole blue cod or snapper – *ask your fishmonger to remove the gut, gills and scales*

100g oregano

1 lemon, *thinly sliced*

1 tsp sea salt

¼ tsp pepper

3 tbsp Pukara extra-virgin olive oil

whole fish

Preheat the oven to 200°C. Run a sharp knife lightly down the length of the fish twice on each side to create score marks; this will help it to cook evenly and stops the skin from tearing during cooking. Mix together the oregano and lemon in a small bowl with the salt and pepper. Divide the mix in two and stuff the gut cavity of each fish. Place the fish onto a baking tray and drizzle with olive oil. Roast in the oven for 15–18 minutes or until cooked.

2 tbsp Pukara extra-virgin olive oil

4 shallots, sliced

150ml white wine

1 small fresh red chilli, *sliced (optional)*

1kg mixed cleaned shellfish, *e.g. cockles and green-lipped mussels*

3 tbsp Worcestershire sauce

1 lemon, *cut into wedges*

2 large tomatoes, *diced*

250g butter

2 tbsp chopped oregano

2 tbsp chopped marjoram

2 tbsp snipped chives

2 tbsp chopped parsley

shellfish and spicy tomato fumet

Heat the olive oil to a shimmer in a saucepan. Add the shallots and sauté for 4 minutes or until the shallots are translucent. In a large saucepan, combine the cooked shallots, wine and chilli and bring to the boil. Add the shellfish and steam, covered, for 4–5 minutes until all the shellfish have opened — discard any that remain closed. Remove the shellfish from the saucepan and set aside. Bring the liquid used to cook the shellfish to the boil and add the remaining ingredients, stirring until well combined and a rich sauce is created. Remove from the heat.

2 small dinner rolls

6 tsp Pukara extra-virgin olive oil

bread garnish

Cut each bread roll in half lengthways, brush with the oil on both sides and toast in the oven until golden and crunchy.

assembly

Place the fish on serving plates. Spoon the fumet on and over the fish, and serve with a sliced and toasted bread roll on the side.

SERVES 2

ROASTED CHICKEN WITH MANCHEGO & SAGE STUFFING

Manchego is a sheep's milk cheese that is gaining popularity in New Zealand. Produced in the La Mancha region, it is probably Spain's most famous cheese. The cheese is aged in natural caves for not less than two months. It has a distinctive, traditional herringbone design on the rind, created by the pressing process, which replicates the pattern created by the wrapping of woven grass in earlier times. Like Parmigiano-Reggiano, Manchego is protected by its Denominacion de Origen, i.e. it is name-controlled, which provides a guarantee of a minimum of two months cave aging. Typically the maturity of Manchego sold in New Zealand is three months but some aged for 12 months is now available. If you are unable to source Manchego, replace it with Pecorino Sardo or Parmigiano-Reggiano.

½ **medium onion,** *finely chopped*

½ **stalk celery,** *chopped*

70g **butter**

6 **slices white toast bread,** *crusts on, cubed*

1 tsp **ground black pepper**

2 **eggs,** *beaten*

½ **cup grated Manchego cheese**

½ tsp **salt**

4 tsp **finely chopped fresh sage** *or 1 tsp dried sage*

1 **size 20 (2kg) whole chicken,** *wing tips removed*

salt and pepper

1 **medium-sized carrot,** *roughly chopped*

1 **medium-sized onion,** *roughly chopped*

6 **cloves garlic,** *peeled*

3 **sprigs of thyme**

2 **sprigs of rosemary**

stuffing

Sauté the onion and celery in the butter until softened. Transfer the onion mixture to a large mixing bowl and combine with the bread, pepper, eggs, grated cheese, salt and sage. Stir together until well moistened. Stuff the cavity of the chicken with the stuffing, then season the skin with salt and pepper.

assembly

Preheat the oven to 220°C. Scatter the carrot and onion in a large ovenproof dish with a lid (or use a large ovenproof frying pan with tin foil as a lid). Add the garlic, thyme and rosemary and set the stuffed chicken on top. Bake for 2 hours, removing the lid or cover in the last 15 minutes to allow the bird to brown. Test to see if the chicken is cooked by inserting a skewer between the breast and the leg. If the juices run clear, it is cooked. Remove from the oven and allow to rest in a warm place for 15 minutes before carving and serving.

SIMON SAYS *For best results, cook the chicken at 220°C and allow 45 minutes per kg, plus 20 minutes. There is always the cheap and cheerful chicken option, but for the best flavour it is worth paying a little more for a corn-fed, organic or free-range chicken. The flesh will be less spongy because a bird that has been allowed to forage free will have built up muscle tone.*

SERVES 4

cocktails & tapas

SNOW BEAN, CAPSICUM & PROSCIUTTO ROULADE

1 red capsicum
salt

capsicum
Preheat the oven to 180°C. Cut the capsicum in half and remove the core and seeds. Season with salt and place the halves on a greased oven tray and roast for 20 minutes. Remove from the oven and place the roasted halves in a plastic ziplock bag or in a bowl covered with cling film. Set aside for 15 minutes or until cool enough to handle, then peel off the skin and slice each half lengthways into six strips.

4 large snow beans or 8 green beans

snow beans
Add some salt to a medium-sized saucepan half full of water and bring to the boil. Place the snow beans in the boiling water to blanch for 1 minute, remove and refresh in a bowl full of iced water. Strain the water and set the beans aside.

3 slices Prosciutto di Parma
Saporoso aged balsamic vinegar

assembly
Preheat the oven to 180°C. Place three slices of prosciutto on the bench so they are lying flat and slightly overlapping to form a large mat. Place three snow beans crossways across the bottom of the prosciutto so that the beans protrude from both ends. Arrange the roasted capsicum ribbons on top of the beans, followed by the fourth snow bean. Roll up the contents tightly in the prosciutto. Bake the roll on an oven tray lined with baking paper for 8 minutes. Remove from the oven and cut into 6–8 pieces. Arrange the pieces on a serving platter with some standing up and some lying down. Serve with Saporoso aged balsamic.

MAKES 1 ROULADE (6–8 PIECES)

PARMESAN & PORCINI MUSHROOM CUSTARD WITH CROSTINI ANTIPASTO PLATTER

Why are porcini mushrooms not grown here in New Zealand? Throughout autumn they seem to grow like weeds in many Italian pine forests. They grow to an incredible size — up to 25cm across — but regrettably by the time they reach that size they are generally full of worms. In France they are known as cèpe de Bordeaux, and in the United Kingdom as cep. Heaven knows we have enough pine forests in this country; surely we could grow them? Meanwhile, these little custards are perfect served as a hot side dish with chicken or beef as well as making a great sandwich spread with smoked chicken.

50g garlic cloves, *peeled*
½ cup chicken stock
1 tbsp butter
½ cup milk
1 cup cream
60g porcini paste
50g Parmigiano-Reggiano
1 tsp porcini powder
2 eggs
1 egg yolk
salt and pepper
1 tbsp olive oil or canola spray, *for greasing the moulds*

custard

Preheat the oven to 150°C. Fill a small saucepan with 500ml of water. Drop the garlic cloves into the pan, bring to the boil and simmer for 2 minutes. Using a slotted spoon, remove the garlic, replace the water and repeat the process, discarding the water the second time around. Pour the chicken stock into the saucepan. Add the butter and the boiled garlic. Simmer until reduced to a syrup comprising approximately 2 tablespoons of liquid. Add the milk and cream and return to the boil. Transfer to a food processor. Add the porcini paste, grated cheese, porcini powder, eggs and egg yolk, salt and pepper. Blend the contents on high for 30 seconds or until a smooth consistency is achieved. Pour into a measuring jug and skim any froth from the top of the mixture. Using oil or spray, grease six dariole moulds, then pour the custard into the moulds to within 1cm of the top of the mould. Place the custards in a deep ovenproof dish and add water to come halfway up the sides of the custard moulds. Cover the dish with tin foil and bake for 60 minutes. until the custards are set. Remove the custards from the oven and cool on a rack for 20 minutes. Transfer to the refrigerator until chilled. When required, run a small knife around the inside of each mould and turn upside down to release the custard onto the serving platter.

6 slices fresh ciabatta *(about half a loaf)*
2 tbsp olive oil

crostini

Brush both sides of the ciabatta slices with olive oil and place on an oven tray. Toast in a preheated 180°C oven for 10 minutes.

125g buffalo mozzarella
6 giant green olives
6 semi-dried tomatoes

antipasto

Cut the mozzarella into bite-sized pieces and arrange in a bowl with the olives and semi-dried tomatoes.

6 pieces cooked porcini *(optional)*
1 tsp Pukara extra-virgin olive oil
½ cup almonds

assembly

Place a custard, topped with a slice of cooked porcini, on a large platter. Drizzle 1 teaspoon of olive oil on the platter and arrange the crostini, antipasto bowl and almonds to one side.

special equipment *6 dariole moulds*

MAKES 6 CUSTARDS (1 PER ANTIPASTO PLATTER)

APEROL SPRITZ

Aperol is a red-to orange-coloured Italian aperitif with a bittersweet orange and herb taste achieved through a blend of bitter orange, gentian, rhubarb and an array of herbs and roots. First produced in 1919 by Barbieri in Padua, it is currently produced by Campari and its fame has spread worldwide. It's a great aperitif — only 11% alcohol per volume — and one that the ladies love. While it's not yet readily available in New Zealand, its time will come, I am sure.

30ml Aperol
prosecco *(a dry sparkling wine from northern Italy)*
1 orange slice
1 piece lemon peel

Half-fill a tumbler with ice, add the Aperol then fill almost to the top with prosecco. Add the orange slice and lemon peel.

SERVES 1

KENTUCKY HIGHBALL
see page 179

PASHA WHISKEY SOUR

The Whiskey Sour is probably the most popular of all the sour drinks and rightfully so. It is a great cocktail. It is sour, yes, but the sweetness of the bourbon and sugar syrup offsets the tartness, especially when using the sweeter bourbons. There are many variations; my favourite is one served by barman extraordinaire Jonas Malig. His variation brings out the oils from the lime wedges and adds another dimension.

3 lemon wedges
3 lime wedges
10ml sugar syrup *(see page 232)*
60ml Chivas Regal 12-year-old
1 egg white
lemon or lime wheels

Place the lemon and lime wedges and the sugar syrup in a Boston shaker. Lightly muddle (see page 179), add the Chivas Regal and the egg white. Fill the shaker with ice, then shake vigorously for 30 seconds. Pour into an old-fashioned or rock glass. Garnish with lemon or lime wheels.

SERVES 1

MYAGHI MULE

This recipe is unashamedly stolen from Simon McGoram, one of Auckland's leading barmen. Easy to make, it's a classic cocktail with readily available ingredients that is refreshing on the palate with a unique flavour. The ginger and wasabi components may sound a little extreme, but trust me: this is an any-time cocktail with personality.

6 long strips cucumber peel
1 tsp wasabi paste
10ml sugar syrup *(see page 232)*
45ml Zubrowka Bison Grass Polish vodka
15ml fresh lime juice
1 small bottle ginger beer
½ cherry tomato

Muddle the cucumber with the wasabi. Add the sugar syrup, vodka and lime juice, shake in an ice-filled Boston shaker and strain into a highball glass over ice. Top up with ginger beer. Garnish with a slice of unpeeled cucumber folded on a toothpick and half a cherry tomato.

SIMON SAYS *Muddle is pressing together certain cocktail ingredients, usually in the bottom of a mixing glass, with a special bar tool known as a muddler, before adding the liquid ingredients.*

SERVES 1

KENTUCKY HIGHBALL

Another of Auckland's top barmen, Thiago Vieira, offered me this great cocktail for the book — and so he should, given the practice he's had in perfecting the mix while making them for me. Characterised by the Wild Turkey bourbon with its wood and caramel notes, it's a masculine drink, refreshing and boosting — and it has the advantage of being easy to construct at home. Experiment by substituting a fruity liqueur, especially an orange or stone fruit one, in place of the sugar syrup.

7 mint leaves
15ml sugar syrup *(see page 232)*
30ml fresh lime juice or lemon juice
45ml Wild Turkey bourbon
soda water

Place the mint and sugar syrup in a highball glass and gently muddle. Add the lime juice and bourbon, fill the glass with crushed ice and stir slowly, bringing the mint from the bottom to the middle. Top up with soda water.

SERVES 1

PIZZA WITH GORGONZOLA DOLCE, CABERNET PEAR, CIPOLLINE ONION, MOZZARELLA, WALNUTS & WHITE BALSAMIC–DRESSED ROCKET

Pizza used to be eaten by the working man and his family because it was a thrifty and convenient food. Nowadays it doesn't often possess either of those attributes. In fact, I can think of no other food that has been so brutalised and titivated to tempt the market. Interestingly, the recipe below could be criticised for the same reasons were it not for the fact that it holds true to the Neapolitan-style thin crust and basically simple toppings.

cabernet pear

1 pear
1½ cups sugar
2 cups water
2 cups cabernet sauvignon
1 stick cinnamon
2 star anise

Peel the pear and core it from the bottom. Combine the sugar, water, cabernet, cinnamon and star anise in a small saucepan and bring to the boil. Reduce the heat, stand the pear in the cabernet poaching liquor and cover the pan with a lid. Simmer for 20–30 minutes or until the pear is tender. Remove the pear from the cooking liquid , allow it to cool, then slice vertically. Set aside until required.

pizza dough

4g compressed yeast
1½ tsp sugar
57ml warm water
133g Tipo 00 pizza flour
1½ tsp salt
3 tbsp olive oil

Dissolve the yeast and sugar in the warm water. Place the flour and salt in the mixer bowl with a dough hook. Work at a low speed, slowly adding the yeast and water mixture and 2 tablespoons of the olive oil. Mix until the dough forms a ball and is slightly sticky (about 8 minutes). Turn the dough on to a floured surface and knead by hand for 2 minutes further until it forms a smooth, round ball. Use the last tablespoon of oil to grease a large bowl, then place the dough in the bowl. Cover with plastic wrap and leave to rise in a warm, draught-free area until it doubles in size (about 30–35 minutes).

onions

5 cipolline onions in oil
150ml cipolline onion juice

Slice the cipolline onions. Place them and the juice in a small saucepan and reduce over low heat until almost no juice is left. Set aside to cool before use.

Gorgonzola Dolce sauce

1 tbsp olive oil
1 tbsp onion, *finely chopped*
6g butter
6g flour
5 tbsp milk
15g Gorgonzola Dolce
salt and pepper

Heat the olive oil in a sauté pan and sauté the onion until it is translucent. Remove from the heat and set aside. Melt the butter in a small saucepan over a medium heat. When melted, remove from the heat and add the flour. Using a wooden spoon, mix the butter and flour until they are well combined and resemble soft breadcrumbs. Cook the flour and butter over a low heat for 1 minute, taking care not to allow the flour to colour. Remove from the heat and begin adding the milk, just a dribble initially, mixing it in to produce a stiff dough. Keep adding milk and mixing it in so that a progressively thinner dough results, a smooth runny batter is achieved. Begin cooking and thickening. Cook for 20 minutes, stirring and taking care to prevent any catching. Finally stir in the Gorgonzola, season to taste and allow to cool before use.

1 clove garlic, *diced*

3 tbsp diced onion

1 tbsp olive oil

1 tsp tomato paste

1 tbsp red wine

5 large Italian-style canned whole peeled tomatoes

70ml juice from tomatoes

1 tbsp chopped basil

1 tbsp chopped thyme

1 tbsp chopped oregano

1 tsp vegetable stock powder

2 tsp brown sugar

salt and pepper

flour

herb or flaky salt and pepper

30g mozzarella cheese, *sliced*

1 small bunch rocket

2 tsp Pukara extra-virgin olive oil

2 tsp white balsamic vinegar

15 walnut halves

20g Gorgonzola Dolce, *cut into 6 small pieces*

special equipment *30–35cm pizza pan or baking tray*

pizza sauce

In a sauté pan, sauté the garlic and onion in the olive oil over a low to medium heat for 5 minutes until they become translucent. Add the tomato paste and cook for 2 minutes. Add the red wine and reduce by half, then add the peeled tomatoes and tomato juice. Bring to the boil and simmer for 10 minutes, then add the chopped herbs. Simmer for a further 5 minutes. Transfer the mixture to a high-speed blender, add the stock powder and brown sugar, then purée to a smooth consistency. Return the sauce to a saucepan and bring back to the boil. Remove from the heat, season to taste and set aside to cool before use.

assembly

Preheat the oven to 200°C (on fanbake). Sprinkle some flour on the kitchen bench and roll out the pizza dough to approximately 30–35cm in diameter. Grease the pizza pan or baking tray with a little olive oil and lay the pizza dough over it. Spoon the Gorgonzola Dolce sauce over the pizza dough, spreading it evenly with the back of the spoon. Arrange slices of the cabernet pear and cipolline onions and a few tablespoons of pizza sauce on top, then sprinkle with herb or flaky salt and some pepper. Bake the pizza for 7 minutes, remove from the oven and scatter the mozzarella on top before returning it to the oven to bake for about 4 minutes until golden on the sides. While the pizza is cooking, dress the rocket with the olive oil and white balsamic vinegar. Remove the pizza from the oven and brush the edges with olive oil. Scatter the walnuts and Gorgonzola over the hot pizza, followed by the dressed rocket. Serve immediately.

SIMON SAYS *The Italian word* dolce *means sweet. In the context of Gorgonzola, it conveys a less strong blue than Piccante. Prepare the cabernet pear a day in advance, leaving the pears to soak in the liquor after cooking and prior to slicing.*

MAKES 1 LARGE PIZZA

PIZZA WITH HAND-ROLLED SAVOURY MEATBALLS, GORGONZOLA PICCANTE, SLICED TOMATO, MOZZARELLA & PROSCIUTTO

Many years ago, Mamma found she had no mince for the lasagne at the last minute. Knowing that Papa and the boys would be in for lunch shortly, desperate measures were called for. A quick round-up of tasty leftover meats were rolled into balls and placed between the pasta sheets and the problem was solved. Respectful of this Italian ingenuity, I decided to try this as part of the topping for a pizza. The results would have made Mamma proud and our restaurant pizza aficionados have also given it the thumbs up.

1 clove garlic, *diced*
½ medium onion, *diced*
1 tbsp olive oil
1 tsp tomato paste
1 tbsp red wine
5 large peeled tomatoes, *roughly chopped*
70ml tomato juice
1 tbsp chopped basil
1 tbsp chopped thyme
1 tbsp chopped oregano
1 tsp vegetable stock powder
2 tsp brown sugar
salt and pepper

4g fresh yeast
57ml warm water
1½ tsp sugar
133g pizza flour
1½ tsp salt
3 tbsp olive oil

15g Prosciutto di Parma, *minced*
15g minced pork cheek or pork mince
10g spicy salami, *minced*
salt and pepper

2 small tomatoes, *sliced*
herb or flaky salt and ground pepper
20g Gorgonzola Piccante
30g mozzarella, *preferably fresh buffalo mozzarella*
1 slice Prosciutto di Parma, *cut into strips*

special equipment *30–35cm pizza pan or baking tray*

pizza sauce

In a sauté pan, sauté the garlic and onion in the olive oil over a low–medium heat for 5 minutes until they become translucent. Add the tomato paste and cook for 2 minutes. Add the red wine and reduce by half, then add the peeled tomatoes and tomato juice. Bring to the boil and simmer for 10 minutes, then add the chopped herbs. Simmer for a further 5 minutes. Transfer the mixture to a high-speed blender, add the stock powder and brown sugar, then purée to a smooth consistency. Return the sauce to a saucepan and bring back to the boil. Remove from the heat, season to taste and set aside to cool.

pizza dough

Dissolve the yeast in the warm water and sugar. Place the flour and salt in a mixer bowl with a dough hook. Work at a low speed, slowly adding the yeast and water mixture and 2 tablespoons of the olive oil. Mix until the dough forms a ball and is slightly sticky (about 8 minutes). Turn out the dough on a floured surface and knead by hand for 2 further minutes until it forms a smooth, round ball. Use the last tablespoon of oil to grease a large bowl, then place the dough in it. Cover with cling film and leave to rise in a warm, draught-free area until it doubles in size (about 30–35 minutes).

meatballs

Place all the minced meat in a bowl and mix together. Season, then roll the mixture into small balls by hand and set aside.

assembly

Preheat the oven to 200°C (on fan bake). Sprinkle some flour on the bench and roll out the pizza dough to approximately 30–35cm in diameter. Grease the pizza pan or baking tray with a little olive oil and lay the pizza dough over it. Spread a coating of pizza sauce over the dough, then arrange the tomato slices and meatballs on top. Season with salt and pepper. Bake for 7 minutes, then remove from the oven and scatter the Gorgonzola Piccante and mozzarella on top before returning it to the oven to bake for about 4 minutes until golden on the sides. Remove the pizza from the oven and brush the edges with olive oil. Drape the strips of prosciutto over the pizza and serve.

SIMON SAYS *If you do not have a mincer, place the meatball ingredients a food processor and process until they are almost a paste.*

MAKES 1 LARGE PIZZA

GRISSINI STICKS WITH ROCKET & FIG MARSALA WRAPPED IN BELLOTA GRAN RESERVA

The Italians have their wonderful Prosciutto di Parma and the Spanish take justifiable pride in their jamón ibérico. The Iberian pig is dark in colour, with little or no hair and a lean body — a much smaller animal than the Italian animal raised for prosciutto. The finest jamón ibérico is called jamón ibérico de bellota (acorn). This ham is from free-range pigs that roam oak forests — each animal needs a full hectare to adequately sustain itself without supplementary feeding. Bellota Gran Reserva is the king of the ibéricos and is aged for 30–40 months. The cured meat varies from red to pale pink in colour, is flecked with delicious fat and has an intense aroma. Initially, it tastes slightly sweet, a sensation that intensifies as the fat melts, giving way to an unbelievably rich flavour. Before you flip the page and write off jamón ibérico because of its fat content, take heed. Because of the pig's diet of acorns, much of the jamón's fat is oleic acid, an unsaturated fatty acid that has been shown to lower LDL ('bad') cholesterol and raise HDL ('good') cholesterol. In any event, there is little danger of overindulging since a kilo of this delicacy will probably cost you more than your first car. Jamón should be cut as thinly as possible and served at room temperature.

200ml lukewarm water

25g compressed yeast

500g Italian 00 baking flour *(see page 236)*

90ml Pukara extra-virgin olive oil

15g salt

1 egg yolk

grissini

Preheat the oven to 160°C. Put half the lukewarm water in a small bowl, sprinkle the yeast over it and leave it to stand for 2 minutes to soften. Whisk with a fork to dissolve the yeast, then let it stand for a further 5 minutes to activate. Put the flour, olive oil, yeast mix, salt and egg yolk in an electric mixer bowl. Mix with a dough hook to a crumbly texture. Slowly and progressively add the remaining lukewarm water and continue to mix until the dough is soft and elastic. Turn out the dough on the bench, form into a ball and cover with a clean, damp tea towel. Leave to prove until nearly double in size. Using a palette knife, cut off small pieces of dough one by one, pulling and stretching each piece to measure around 25–30cm in length and the thickness of a pen. Place the dough lengths on an oiled oven tray and bake for 8–10 minutes or until lightly golden. Remove from the oven and allow to cool, before storing in an airtight container.

SIMON SAYS *The addition of 4 tablespoons of grated Parmigiano-Reggiano after the lukewarm water makes for a great grissini that can stand alone.*

12 slices jamón ibérico de bellota Gran Reserva

30g fig marsala *(see page 239 Salsafichi)*

small bunch of rocket

special equipment *electric mixer with dough hook*

assembly

Lay out the ham slices on a clean chopping board or bench top and spread the fig marsala compote evenly over each slice. Divide the rocket into 12 portions and position one at the end of each slice. Nestle a grissini stick in the rocket and tightly roll up the ham to enclose the rocket and the grissini. Repeat to make 12 wrapped grissini. Serve standing in a tall glass.

SERVES 6 WITH EXTRA GRISSINI LEFT OVER

COCKTAIL & TAPAS

CLEVEDON OYSTERS GRILLED WITH MANDARIN & JALAPEÑO

These are great done under the grill or on the barbecue. Not that one ever needs an excuse to eat oysters, but recent research, has shown more important health benefits from oysters beyond the mythical nonsense associated with libido. My motivation for the regular inclusion of oysters in my diet is purely because of their ability to lower serum cholesterol. Japanese studies have shown that the consumption of oysters can reduce the onset and symptoms of heart disease, which is thought to stem from their high taurine and hypotaurine levels.

18 mandarin segments
18 large Clevedon half-shell oysters
1½ tsp Tabasco green pepper (*jalapeño*)
   sauce
1 tsp mandarin-infused oil

Slice the mandarin segments in half lengthways. Loosen and remove the oysters from their shells and discard any loose shell debris. Place a slice of mandarin inside each shell and top with an oyster. Drizzle with the Tabasco green pepper (*jalapeño*) sauce and mandarin-infused oil. Divide the extra slices of mandarin between the oysters.

assembly
Preheat the grill to medium. Arrange the oysters on a suitable oven tray and place under the preheated grill for 5 minutes. The oysters should be only just hot in the middle. Turn down the bed and serve.

NATURAL CLEVEDON OYSTERS WITH WHITE BALSAMIC PEARLS

For this presentation of oysters I have employed the El Bulli Texturas magic. The Prelibato white balsamic caviar, which can be made up to three hours in advance, is a stunning taste explosion and this alone will elevate you to 'kitchen legend' status overnight.

70ml water
30g caster sugar
100ml Prelibato white balsamic vinegar
50ml mineral water
4g Texturas Algin
500ml still mineral water
3.4g Texturas Calcic

4 limes, *cut into 3mm slices*
18 Clevedon oysters or rock oysters
1 tsp Oscìetre caviar *(optional)*
30g caviar

special equipment *Texturas syringe, Texturas spoon*

white balsamic caviar balls

Place the water and caster sugar into a small saucepan and simmer for 2 minutes. Allow to cool. Pour the cooled sugar syrup, the balsamic and the first portion of mineral water into a high-speed food processor, then add the Algin. Blend at the highest possible speed for 30 seconds. Pass the mix through a fine sieve into a 1 litre container and allow it to settle for 30 minutes. Using a dessertspoon, carefully remove the white residue from the top of the mix. Pour the still mineral water and the Calcic into the high-speed food processor and process until the Calcic has dissolved. Pour into another 1 litre container and allow to stand for 1 hour so that the air in the Calcic water dissipates. Fill a Texturas syringe with the balsamic mix and expel, drop by drop into the Calcic bath. Let the balls sit in the Calcic bath for 3 minutes before removing with a Texturas spoon.

assembly

Arrange the lime slices on the plate, one slice per oyster shell, to form a base for the oysters and prevent them from sliding around while being transported to the table. Place a few caviar balls on top of each oyster with some oscìetre caviar. Serve with your favourite chilled vodka or a glass of Gosset champagne.

dessert

WARM CHOCOLATE PUDDING WITH AFTER DINNER MINT ICE CREAM

Cacao beans were so valuable in ancient Mexico that the Maya and subsequent Aztec and Toltec civilisations used them as a means of currency to pay for commodities and taxes. Maybe things have become more sophisticated, but how often do we still try to buy our way out of trouble with chocolate? In any event, this pudding with its runny centre is a chocolate lover's dream.

5 eggs
5 yolks
110 sugar
250g dark chocolate *(at least 72% cocoa solids)*
250g butter
25g flour
2 tbsp cocoa powder

chocolate pudding

Using an electric beater, whisk the eggs and egg yolks with the sugar until thick and pale. Melt the chocolate and butter over a bain-marie, stirring constantly to prevent burning. Fold the melted chocolate mixture into the beaten eggs and sugar until the combination is of an even consistency. Sift the flour over the mix and fold in until completely incorporated and there are no lumps. Transfer the mixture to a piping bag and place in the refrigerator until firm. Grease six dariole moulds and lightly dust with cocoa powder. Once firm, pipe the mixture into the moulds, then set aside.

12 egg yolks
200g sugar
800ml full cream milk
pinch of salt
6 after dinner mints, *preferably Cadbury's, roughly chopped*
200ml cream

ice cream

Using an electric beater, beat the egg yolks and sugar until smooth and creamy. Pour the milk into a medium-sized saucepan and add the salt. Place over a medium heat until just before it begins to simmer, then remove from the heat and leave to stand for 5–10 minutes (do not let it reach simmering stage). While the mixture is standing, prepare an ice-water bath in a bowl large enough to accommodate the bowl that will contain the mixture. Whisk 1 cup of milk in a slow stream into the yolk mixture to temper it, then whisk in another cup, along with the after dinner mints. Transfer the egg yolk mixture to the saucepan with the remaining milk. Cook over a medium–high heat, stirring constantly, until the mixture is thick enough to coat the back of a wooden spoon (run a finger down the back of the coated spoon; if the mixture doesn't run but stays in place on the spoon, it is thick enough). Remove from the heat and mix in the cream to stop the mixture from overcooking. Pour the custard through a medium-mesh sieve into the bowl waiting in the ice-water bath. Allow it to cool completely, stirring regularly until it is completely chilled. Freeze in a Pacojet or use an ice cream machine and churn following the manufacturer's instructions.

6 tuiles *(see page 233)*
icing sugar for dusting
6 orange wafers *(see page 232)*

special equipment 6 dariole moulds (if dariole moulds are not available, small soufflé moulds or coffee cups are suitable), thermometer (optional), ice cream machine or Pacojet

assembly

Preheat the oven to 210°C. Place the chocolate puddings on an oven tray and bake for 12 minutes. Remove from the oven and, very importantly, allow them to stand for 3 minutes before turning them out to avoid cracking. Turn out the puddings onto individual plates, then wedge the wide base of a triangular tuile under each one. Dust with icing sugar; then arrange a scoop of ice cream on each pudding and decorate with an orange wafer.

SERVES 6

CRÈME BRÛLÉE WITH A CHOCOLATE GRAPPA MARBLE & MANDARIN TEA AIR

250ml cream
250ml milk
1 large fresh vanilla bean
7 egg yolks
80g caster sugar

crème brûlée

Preheat the oven to 130°C. In a saucepan, bring the cream and milk to simmering point (about 80°C if you have a sugar thermometer). Using a sharp-pointed vegetable knife, carefully slice along the length of the vanilla bean to open it and to expose the seeds. Remove the saucepan from the heat, scrape the vanilla seeds into the warm milk, then add the pod. Allow the mixture to infuse for 10 minutes. In a bowl, combine the egg yolks and caster sugar and whisk the mixture until thick (this will take a little effort, but the end result is well worth it). Remove the vanilla pod and set aside for further use (see Simon Says). Pour about one-quarter of the cream and vanilla bean mix into the whisked egg and sugar, and whisk to combine. Repeat until all the cream and vanilla bean mix is incorporated (doing it one-quarter at a time ensures that the egg yolks don't cook too quickly, leaving little bits of sweet scrambled egg through the mixture). Strain the mixture through a fine sieve and place in the refrigerator to chill for at least 2 hours. When ready to cook them, divide the chilled mixture between six ramekins and carefully place them into a baking dish and fill with enough hot water to reach halfway up the ramekins. Cover tightly with tin foil and bake for 65 minutes. After 45 minutes carefully remove the tin foil to check the doneness of the custards by giving them a gentle shake (take great care when removing the tin foil to avoid the hot steam); they should have a soft, jelly-like wobble. If slightly underdone and still too liquid, cover and return to the oven, checking every 5 minutes. When they are cooked, remove the dish from the oven and allow the ramekins to cool in the water for 10 minutes before transferring them to the refrigerator for at least 2 hours or until ready to serve.

SIMON SAYS *Thoroughly wash the vanilla pod under cold water then allow to completely dry. Add it to the sugar container to give the sugar a nice vanilla aroma.*

500ml mineral water
3.2g Texturas Calcic
100ml chocolate grappa liqueur
50ml sugar syrup *(see page 232)*
50ml mineral water
1.6g Texturas Algin

chocolate grappa sphere

Pour the first measure of mineral water into the bowl of a blender and sprinkle in the Calcic. Blend until all the little balls of Calcic have dissolved in the solution. Transfer to a clean bowl; this will be the Calcic bath. Clean the blender bowl and add the chocolate grappa, sugar syrup, the second measure of mineral water and the Algin. Blend for 2 minutes, then strain the mixture through a fine sieve into a small container. Give the container a good tap or two on the bench to remove any air bubbles, then leave it to stand for at least 2 hours tapping it again every 30 minutes to remove any remaining air bubbles. Very carefully ease teaspoonfuls of the chocolate grappa mix into the Calcic bath, a process that will create small, marble-shaped spheres. Make two at a time and allow them to mature in the Calcic bath for 2 minutes, during which time an outer skin will form on them. Using the Texturas spoon, carefully lift out each sphere, one at a time, rinsing them in fresh mineral water, then placing on the Texturas holding spoon until ready to serve. Make six spheres in total.

2 tbsp good-quality maple syrup
125g caster sugar
3 tbsp corn syrup or liquid glucose
3 tbsp chilled water

maple caramel wafer

Preheat the oven to 180°C. Over a moderate heat, bring all the ingredients to a very gentle simmer and cook until the mixture reaches a light golden caramel colour (or a 160°C on the sugar thermometer). Give the saucepan a gentle swirl every minute or so, but avoid actually stirring because this will cause the mixture to crystallise. Remove the pan from the heat to prevent further browning. Pour the caramel onto a tray lined with a Teflon baking sheet and leave it to cool and set. Once cool, break the caramel into small pieces, then reduce to a fine crumb in the food processor. Sprinkle the caramel crumb back onto the lined baking tray (if desired, use a cut-out template to create interesting shapes). Place in the oven, for 3–4 minutes or until the caramel softens and melts. Remove from the oven and leave to sit for 1 minute, then using a spatula carefully lift the soft caramel from the paper and drape the shapes over a glass or rolling pin to form a curve as they set.

Note: Take great care when working with hot sugar; it can cause serious burns.

250ml mineral water
1 tsp loose Earl Grey tea
60ml Monin mandarin syrup
1.2g Texturas Lecite

mandarin tea air

Bring the mineral water to a gentle boil and add the tea and mandarin syrup. Give the liquid a swirl or two to combine and allow it to cool. Strain through a fine sieve into a high-sided container and add the Lecite. Create foam, using a hand blender at a 20–30° angle, using a pulsing and lifting action in order to froth the mixture. Gently lift the hand blender clear of the container and allow the foamed mixture to stabilise for 2 minutes before use.

6 tbsp caster sugar

assembly

Sprinkle the caster sugar evenly over each of the six ramekins, then carefully apply a kitchen blowtorch in a sweeping motion to melt and caramelise the sugar. Allow to sit for 2 minutes before arranging a chocolate grappa sphere on one side of each brûlée, with a scoop of mandarin tea air in the centre and a maple caramel wafer to finish.

SERVES 6

special equipment sugar thermometer,
   six ovenproof ramekins, Texturas tool kit,
   kitchen blowtorch

POACHED MELON WITH GIN & TONIC SORBET, LEMON SPHERE & RASPBERRY BALSAMIC

The lemon sphere used here is purely for presentation and is optional. If preferred, serve the lemon curd as a sauce. The gin sorbet is also great as an intermediate course.

1 rock melon
2.5 litres sugar syrup *(see page 232)*
2 cardamom pods
5 juniper berries
½ lemon, *sliced*

poached melon

Peel the melon, remove both ends and slice into five even rounds. Remove and discard the seeds from each round. Combine the sugar syrup, cardamom, juniper berries and lemon slices in a saucepan and bring to the boil. Place the melon rounds in the liquid and remove from the heat. Set aside for 8–10 minutes, then gently remove the melon, strain and allow it to cool.

¾ cup sugar
½ cup water
zest of 1 lemon
1 cup tonic water
1 egg white
juice of 2 lemons
¼ cup gin

gin and tonic sorbet

Combine the sugar, water and lemon zest in a saucepan and bring to the boil. Simmer for 8 minutes, then remove from the heat and allow to cool. Add the tonic water, egg white, juice and gin, and place in an ice cream machine and follow the manufacturer's instructions or place in a Pacojet canister and follow the manufacturer's instructions.

175g caster sugar
3 whole eggs, *separated*
170ml lemon juice
175g butter, *at room temperature*
3.2g Texturas Calcic
1g Texturas Citras
3.2g Texturas Algin
1 litre still mineral water

lemon sphere

In a bain-marie (or a bowl over a saucepan of simmering water), whisk together the sugar and the egg yolks. The water should be simmering gently, not boiling, and the bowl containing the egg mixture should not be in contact with the simmering water. When the mixture is quite foamy, continue whisking and add the lemon juice, one spoonful at a time. Keep whisking until the sauce thickens and becomes a light, foamy custard (about 10 minutes). After the lemon juice has been added, the heat can be increased slightly. Transfer the mixture to a blender, and with the motor running slowly, add the butter. The mixture will begin to thicken and is ready to use as a sauce at this stage. If making spheres, add the Calcic and Citras. Transfer the mixture to a clean container and refrigerate to cool. If the curd is too thick, add up to 100ml of cream. Clean the blender bowl and prepare an Algin bath by processing the Algin and 500ml of still mineral water then set it aside.

1 tbsp raspberry balsamic mousse
8 lemon segments

special equipment Texturas tool kit, Pacojet or ice cream machine

assembly

Place a poached melon ring on each plate. Cut the fifth ring into eight pieces and place two on each plate next to the melon ring to form a base for the lemon sphere. Using the Texturas tablespoon measure, spoon a large portion of the lemon curd mix into the Algin bath to form a sphere. Allow it to mature in the bath for approximately 4 minutes, then carefully remove and rinse well in a mineral water bath. Repeat to make four spheres in total. Place a scoop of gin and tonic sorbet inside each melon ring. Arrange a lemon sphere on top of the melon base. If not using spheres, serve the lemon curd in a sauce jug. Garnish with a squiggle of raspberry balsamic mousse and two lemon segments per plate.

SERVES 4

FEIJOA & APPLE CRUMBLE WITH FRENCH TOAST ICE CREAM & MAPLE SYRUP

The feijoa is something of an oddity — I have the feeling it couldn't quite make its mind up as to how it should taste. When ripe it is aromatic yet sweet and the texture ranges from jelly-like to a gritty, buff-coloured flesh nearer the skin. When properly ripe they fall from the branch and from that moment on it is all downhill, in that they spoil very rapidly. Before they fall, visually there is no real clue as to whether they are ripe, so picking them is a lottery and if picked too soon they can be quite bitter. The lesson there is to stand around waiting for them to fall so as to have an iron-clad guarantee that they are ripe. Cooking them as we have done in this recipe is in my view the best approach to enjoying this very different fruit.

crumble mix

35g sliced almonds
35g rolled oats
2 tbsp honey
65g butter
65g caster sugar
125g flour
½ tsp vanilla essence
35g cornflakes
10 mint leaves, *finely sliced*

Preheat the oven to 150°C. Toast the almonds on a flat roasting tray for 5–7 minutes, shaking the tray occasionally to ensure they toast evenly to a pale gold colour. Toast the oats and honey on a separate tray at the same temperature for 8–10 minutes, stirring occasionally. Set aside and allow to cool. In a mixing bowl, cream the butter and sugar. Sift in the flour until a crumbly consistency is reached, then add the vanilla, cornflakes, toasted almonds and honeyed oats. Lastly add the mint. Set aside until required.

feijoa compote

50g butter
1 vanilla bean
1kg feijoas, *peeled and sliced*
500g Granny Smith apples, *peeled, cored and diced*
½ cup caster sugar
1 cinnamon stick

Preheat the oven to 180°C. Melt the butter in a large saucepan over a medium heat but do not allow it to colour, as this will affect the flavour. Using a sharp-pointed vegetable knife, carefully slice along the length of the vanilla bean to expose the seeds and scrape them into the saucepan, along with the bean. Place the feijoas, apples, sugar and cinnamon into the saucepan and cook over a medium heat, stirring occasionally to prevent the fruit from catching, until the feijoas are tender (about 10–15 minutes). Remove the vanilla pod and place the feijoa mix into a 20cm ovenproof dish and cover with the crumble mix. Bake for 20–30 minutes until the crumble turns a rich golden brown. Remove from the oven and keep warm.

french toast ice cream

100g brioche *(see page 230)*
500ml anglaise *(see page 230)*
½ tsp ground cinnamon

Remove and discard the crust from the brioche and cut into 1cm cubes. Soak the cubed brioche in the anglaise for 2 minutes, then remove and strain. Gently toast the strained brioche in a saucepan on a low heat until it takes on a light brown colour. Take care with the level of heat to avoid burning the milk in the anglaise. Place the brioche, anglaise and cinnamon into a blender and pulse until an almost smooth consistency is reached, then pour into an ice cream machine and follow the manufacturer's instructions. Keep frozen until ready to serve. If using a Pacojet, place the anglaise and ground cinnamon into the Pacojet and follow the manufacturer's instructions. Once the mixture is frozen, blend with the Pacojet and fold through the toasted brioche. Keep frozen.

assembly

60ml maple syrup

Place equal portions of crumble onto six serving plates along with a scoop of ice cream and drizzle with the maple syrup.

special equipment *20cm ovenproof dish, Pacojet or ice cream machine*

SERVES 6

WHITE CHOCOLATE PANNA COTTA WITH PINEAPPLE FOAM & BLUEBERRY CAVIAR

This is an attractive-looking and refreshing dessert utilising the El Bulli Texturas magic to transform blueberry syrup into little caviar-like beads that impart an unexpected taste explosion which contrasts with the creaminess of the panna cotta. It's probably more of a summer dessert and is great as something light to conclude a meal.

white chocolate panna cotta

4 leaves gelatine
250ml milk
1 fresh vanilla bean
250ml cream
2 tbsp caster sugar
160g good-quality white chocolate

Soak the gelatine leaves in 200ml of the milk and set aside. Using the pointed tip of a sharp vegetable knife, slice along the length of the vanilla bean to open it up and expose the seeds (reserve the pod to use when steeping the pineapple later on). Scrape the seeds into a saucepan and add the cream, remaining milk and sugar. Bring the mixture in the saucepan to a gentle simmer (about 80°C on a sugar thermometer) and ensure the sugar has completely dissolved. Squeeze the milk from the gelatine leaves, reserving the soaking milk, and stir them into the vanilla cream until dissolved. Remove from the heat and stir in the white chocolate until it, too, is completely dissolved. Add the cold soaking milk and stir; this will help speed up the setting process. Strain the mix through a fine sieve into a pouring jug and refrigerate for 10 minutes, until a skin forms on the surface of the cream. Carefully remove and discard the skin. Divide the mixture between six dariole moulds, stirring frequently during the portioning so that each mould receives an even amount of the vanilla seeds. Refrigerate for 3 hours until set firm.

vanilla-steeped pineapple

½ pineapple, *ripe but firm, peeled and cored*
2 cups caster sugar
2 cups water

Cut the pineapple into quarters, ensuring all fibre and skin has been cut out, then into julienne and set aside in a heatproof bowl. Bring the sugar, water and scraped-out vanilla pod to the boil, make sure the sugar dissolves completely. Carefully pour the hot syrup over the pineapple strips and allow to cool. Carefully strain off the syrup into a jug and set aside. Place the pineapple on a flat plate or tray and set aside until ready to serve.

pineapple foam

3 leaves gelatine
1 cup cold water
500ml vanilla bean pineapple syrup *(from the poached pineapple)*

Soak the gelatine in the cold water and set aside. In a stainless steel saucepan, bring the reserved pineapple poaching syrup to the boil. Squeeze the water from the gelatine leaves and add to the pineapple syrup. Pour the liquid into a whipped cream dispenser or a Whip-it. Charge the vessel with 3–4 canisters and refrigerate for at least 3 hours.

blueberry caviar

500ml mineral water
3.2g Texturas Calcic
100g fresh or frozen blueberries
200ml sugar syrup *(see page 232)*
1.7g Texturas Algin

Pour the mineral water into the bowl of a blender and sprinkle in the Calcic. Blend until all the little balls of Calcic have dissolved. Transfer to a clean bowl; this will be the Calcic bath. Place the blueberries and sugar syrup into a stainless steel saucepan, bring the contents to the boil and set aside to cool. Pour the cooled blueberry and sugar syrup into a blender and process until smooth, add the Algin and process again for 1 minute. Pour the mix through a fine sieve, discarding any solids. Give the bowl containing the mixture a firm tap or two on the bench to remove

any air bubbles, then leave to sit for 2 hours, tapping it occasionally. Load the Texturas syringe with the cooled blueberry mixture and drop small balls of it into the Calcic bath, a little at a time. Leave in the bath for approximately 1 minute. Using the Texturas slotted spoon, carefully remove the blueberry caviar and rinse in fresh water to remove any residue of the Calcic mixture.

special equipment *Texturas tool kit, 6 dariole moulds, whipped cream charger/ Whip-it, thermometer*

assembly
Briefly dip each dariole mould into a bowl of hot water to loosen the panna cotta, then turn out into individual serving bowls. Arrange some poached pineapple on top of each panna cotta. Give the pineapple foam a vigorous shake and pipe a neat ring around each panna cotta. Finish with a small mound of blueberry caviar on top of the pineapple and decorate the pineapple foam with additional caviar.

SERVES 6

PINEAPPLE PANNA COLADA WITH CARAMEL RUM GRANITA & CARPACCIO OF PINEAPPLE WITH SPICY CARAMEL

The Caribe Hilton Hotel in Puerto Rico claims that its bartender, Ramon 'Monchito' Marrero, spent three months perfecting the piña colada recipe in 1954. Several other bars also claim to have invented it. Euro head chef Shane Yardley, who developed this dessert, can rightfully claim he has taken a famous cocktail and a famous dessert and transformed them into a sensational combination. It's worth noting that Shane didn't need as much time as Monchito Marrero to get his recipe right.

200ml water
50g sugar
60ml light rum, *e.g. Appletons or Mt Gay*

rum granita
In a small saucepan, bring the water and sugar to a simmer for 10 minutes. Remove from the heat, add the rum and freeze in a shallow, flat container.

7 leaves gelatine
500ml milk
500ml cream
5 tbsp caster sugar
200g shredded coconut

panna cotta
Place the gelatine leaves into a bowl of cold water. Place the milk, cream, caster sugar and coconut in a saucepan and bring to the boil. Remove from the heat and pass through a fine sieve to remove the coconut, then return the milk and cream to the saucepan and again bring to the boil. Remove from the heat and whisk in the soaked and drained gelatine. Pass once more through a fine sieve into a pouring jug. Pour the mixture into dariole moulds and refrigerate to set.

100g sugar
100g water
100ml cream
10 pink peppercorns

spicy caramel
Place the sugar and water in a small pan and simmer until the mixture caramelises. Place the cream and peppercorns in a small microwaveable container and microwave on high power until almost boiling. Add this to the hot caramel and whisk until the caramel has dissolved. Allow to cool, then strain and discard the peppercorns. Transfer the mixture to a small plastic squeeze bottle with a fine nozzle.

½ pineapple, *peeled*
1 tsp caster sugar

special equipment *6 dariole moulds, small squeeze bottle*

pineapple carpaccio
Preheat the oven to 120°C. Using a meat slicer, slice the pineapple so thinly it is see-through. Cut 24 slices and set aside. Cut one extra slice for the caramelised wafer used to garnish. Divide the extra slice into six and sprinkle with sugar. Lift the pieces with tongs onto a Teflon or non-stick baking sheet and bake for one hour or until completely dried. Remove from the sheet and allow to cool on a flat surface. Store in an airtight container until ready to use.

assembly
Arrange four slices of pineapple carpaccio on each plate. Squeeze out some spicy caramel to make a lattice pattern, then position a panna cotta in the centre. At the last minute, remove the rum granita from the freezer. Use a tablespoon to create shavings to decorate the top of each panna cotta. Garnish with a piece of the caramelised pineapple.

SERVES 6

CHOCOLATE ZEN WITH STRAWBERRY JELLY ON GINGERSNAP CRUNCH

Shane Yardley, head chef at Euro, created this chocolate-based surprise package. The crunchiness of the base is contrasted nicely with the rich soft mousse whilst the hidden strawberry jelly centre adds tartness that contrast well with the rich chocolate elements of this long time favourite. Being able to prepare the servings ahead of time and plate directly from the refrigerator has obvious advantages.

85g hazelnuts, *roasted and peeled*
100g icing sugar
85g egg whites
20g caster sugar
200g Nutella spread
50g white chocolate
30g cornflakes, *crushed*
40g Gingernut biscuits, *crushed*

gingernut base

Preheat the oven to 170°C. In a food processor, blend together the hazelnuts and 85g of the icing sugar to a fine texture. Using an electric beater, whisk the egg whites until soft peaks form. Add the caster sugar and continue to whisk for a further 3–4 minutes until a stiff meringue is achieved. Fold the hazelnut mixture into the meringue. Line a baking tray with baking paper and spread the meringue mix evenly over the paper. Dust with the remaining icing sugar and bake for 6–7 minutes. While the meringue is baking, place the Nutella in a microwaveable bowl, add the white chocolate and heat for 1 minute on high power. Stir, return to the microwave for a further 30 seconds, then remove and stir again. Continue this process until the contents become runny. Add the crushed cornflakes and crushed gingernut biscuits and mix together. Spread evenly over the cooked meringue base and place in the refrigerator to cool.

270g good-quality dark chocolate *(at least 64% cocoa solids)*
335ml cream
165ml water
225g sugar
85g cocoa powder

chocolate ganache

Place the chocolate and 250ml of the cream into a large metal bowl and position over a saucepan of water, taking care that the bottom of the bowl does not touch the simmering water. When the chocolate has melted and combined with the cream, remove from the heat and set aside. In a clean saucepan, bring the water and sugar to the boil. Remove from the heat, whisk in the cocoa powder, then add the remaining cream. Return the pan to the heat and bring back to the boil. Pass the mixture through a fine sieve and then mix with the chocolate ganache. Set aside to cool.

100ml chocolate ganache, *cooled to room temperature*
85g soft-whipped cream

chocolate mousse

Place 100ml of the cooled chocolate ganache into a large bowl. Fold half of the whipped cream into the chocolate mixture. Once combined, fold back into the remaining whipped cream. Chill until required.

200ml water
150g caster sugar
250g frozen strawberries
2 gelatine leaves

strawberry jelly

Pour the water and sugar into a large saucepan and add the strawberries. Bring to the boil and simmer for 4 minutes. Remove from the heat and cover with cling film to cool. Soften the gelatine in cold running water. Strain the strawberry liquor into a clean saucepan and bring back to the boil. When hot, remove from the heat and add the softened gelatine. Stir until the gelatine has dissolved. Allow to cool until not quite set.

orange balsamic mousse
6 chocolate tuiles *(see page 233)*
icing sugar

special equipment *6 x 7cm x 4cm*
moulds, 7cm pastry cutter, piping bag

assembly

Using a 7cm pastry cutter, cut six circles from the gingersnap base. Lightly press the bases into the moulds. Pipe the mousse on top of the bases to reach a height of 4cm. Transfer the filled moulds to the freezer for 3 hours or until frozen.

Using a teaspoon dipped in hot water, scoop out 2 spoonfuls from the centre of each frozen mousse. Reserve the spoonfuls and keep frozen for later use. Pour some cooled jelly into the resulting hole in the top of each mousse. Return the mousses to the freezer so the jelly can set, then place the reserved frozen spoonfuls on top to cover the jelly. Return to the freezer overnight.

When ready to finish, place a large saucepan of water over a high heat and bring to the boil, then reduce to a simmer. Put the remaining chocolate ganache in a large bowl and position it on top of the saucepan of simmering water, taking care that the bottom of the bowl does not touch the water. Stir until the mixture has melted, remove from the heat and set aside. Remove the moulds from the freezer and carefully turn out the frozen mousses. Using a palette knife dipped in hot water, smooth any rough edges. Place the mousses on a wire cake rack positioned over a tray. Spoon the chocolate ganache over the frozen mousses to evenly coat. Transfer to the refrigerator to set. Just before serving, use a pastry brush to paint a line of orange balsamic mousse at one end of each plate. Using a palette knife carefully position a mousse in the centre of each plate. Dust half of a chocolate tuile with icing sugar and carefully insert one end into each mousse.

SERVES 6

BUTTERSCOTCH PUDDING SURROUNDED BY WARM CREAM TOPPED WITH RUM-SPIKED CARAMEL SAUCE

Years ago, in Britain, I pestered my way into a position at Thornbury Castle with Britain's first Michelin star chef Kenneth Bell. It's a time I remember with great fondness, along with gratitude to Kenneth for taking on a 20-year-old Kiwi whose only claim to fame was that he had worked briefly for Prue Leith in London. Shortly after I commenced work at the castle I noticed that Kenneth, in times of stress, was inclined to launch himself from the top of the castle swinging precariously beneath a hang-glider. Rumour had it that he did it more frequently while I was working there. Make of that what you will, but I featured Kenneth's butterscotch pudding recipe on the menu in my first restaurant more than 20 years ago and it's been there ever since.

150g butter
300g sugar
450g self-raising flour
1 tsp baking soda
1½ tsp baking powder
450ml milk
½ tsp vanilla essence
3 eggs
150g each dried apricots, dates and
　prunes
80g blanched almonds

120g butter
250g brown sugar
300ml cream
60ml rum *(Appletons or Mt Gay)*

1200ml cream

pudding

Preheat the oven to 150°C. Cream the butter and sugar until light and fluffy. Mix the flour and baking soda through the butter and sugar. Heat the milk to just before boiling and add the vanilla essence. Carefully mix the hot milk into the creamed butter and sugar mixture. Incorporate the eggs, one at a time, until well mixed. Pour the batter into a greased loaf tin. Scatter the dried fruit and nuts evenly over the surface of the batter, then leave it to sit for 20 minutes. Gently push the fruit and nuts just below the surface of the batter. Bake the pudding until golden brown (about 1 hour 15 minutes–1 hour 30 minutes). Cover and bake for a further 30 minutes or so (2 hours in total).

butterscotch sauce

In a small saucepan, bring the butter, sugar and cream to the boil. Remove from the heat and add the rum, mixing well to combine.

assembly

Cut the pudding into thick slices and warm them in the oven for 5 minutes. Place a slice of pudding in each bowl. Heat the cream until hot, pour it evenly over each portion. Cover generously with the butterscotch sauce.

SERVES 6

SAUTERNES CUSTARD IN A PASSIONFRUIT & FENNEL SOUP

This would have to be my all-time favourite dessert. Sauternes is a French dessert wine from the region of the same name in Bordeaux. While working for Larry Ellison, I was fortunate enough on a couple of occasions to make this dessert with the world's best-ever Sauternes, Château d'Yquem, and it was sensational. Unquestionably one of the finest and most highly sought after dessert wines in the world, in the 1855 official classification of Bordeaux wines, Château d'Yquem was the only sauternais to be accorded the rank of Grand Premier Cru.

caramel

3 tablespoons water
100g sugar
grapeseed oil

Pour the water into a small saucepan. Add the sugar and, over a medium heat, bring the syrup to the boil and simmer until a golden caramel is achieved. Grease each dariole mould with grapeseed oil, pour a tablespoon of caramel into each mould and leave to set.

custard

185ml sauternes
2 eggs
5 egg yolks
75g sugar
350ml cream

Preheat the oven to 140°C. Pour the wine into a saucepan and reduce to 150ml over a low heat. Place the eggs, egg yolks and sugar in a large mixing bowl. Using an electric beater, whip on high speed until the sugar and egg mixture is thick and pale. Add the cream and the reduced wine and stir together. Transfer to the refrigerator to rest for 30 minutes. Skim off any froth that has formed on top of the custard mixture, then pour into the dariole moulds with the caramel in the bottom. Place the moulds into an oven dish and fill with hot water to reach halfway up the sides of the moulds. Cover with tin foil and bake for 35 minutes, until the custard is set. If the custard is still not properly set, leave them in the oven for a little longer. Insert a skewer into the centre of one to test; it should be clean when you remove it. Remove the set custards, still in their moulds, from the water and allow to cool before refrigerating until required.

passionfruit and fennel soup

250ml water
100g sugar
25ml passionfruit pulp
½ tbsp finely diced fennel bulb
10ml Pernod

Pour the water into a medium-sized saucepan and add the sugar. Bring to the boil and simmer for 2 minutes. Add the passionfruit pulp and the diced fennel and simmer for a further 2 minutes. Remove from the heat, add the Pernod and allow to cool.

1 stalk fennel

assembly

Invert a dariole mould onto the centre of each serving bowl. Shake gently to loosen and release the custards. To finish, pour the passionfruit and fennel soup around each custard and pick some fennel leaves from the stalk and drop into the soup.

special equipment *6 dariole moulds*

SIMON SAYS *Making the custards a day in advance produces a better result because the caramel will be runny when the custards are removed from the moulds.*

SERVES 6

ALMOND & BERRY PIE WITH EGG NOG ICE CREAM & CASSIS COULIS

I once borrowed an ice cream maker from my mother. She purchased another one, which in due course I also borrowed because the first one had worn out. Mother purchased yet another one, but for some reason she won't lend it to me. It's probably something I said. If you don't have an ice cream maker, a good quality commercial vanilla ice cream is a most acceptable alternative to serve with this warm pie.

400g plain flour
3 tbsp caster sugar
3 tsp baking powder
200g unsalted butter, *chilled*
½ cup ice-cold water

50g caster sugar
50ml still mineral water
300g blackcurrants *(frozen are acceptable)*
½ cup crème de cassis
150g marzipan

flour
300g marzipan
6 black doris plums *(canned are acceptable)*
6 tablespoons blackcurrants *(frozen are acceptable)*
2 egg yolks
8 tbsp cream

egg nog ice cream *(see page 234)*

special equipment *6 x 8cm stainless pastry rings, 10cm pastry cutter, sugar thermometer*

pastry
In a bowl, mix together the flour, sugar and baking powder. Grate the cold butter into the bowl and add the ice-cold water. Mix well and knead until smooth. Cover the bowl with cling film and refrigerate for 30 minutes.

cassis coulis
Place the caster sugar and mineral water in a saucepan over a moderate heat until the sugar is dissolved. Add the blackcurrants, crème de cassis and marzipan and bring to a slow simmer for 5 minutes. Transfer to a blender and blend until smooth. Set aside until required.

assembly
Preheat the oven to 200°C. Roll out the pastry to 2mm thick on a cold, floured surface, using the extra flour to prevent it from sticking. Using the pastry cutter, cut out six rings and set aside for use as lids. Re-form the remaining pastry and divide the dough into six balls. Roll out each ball to 2mm thick. Line each pastry ring with some pastry, then transfer to the refrigerator for 30 minutes. Divide the marzipan into six pieces and flatten each with your hand so it will neatly fit into the pie base. Cut the plums in half, removing the stones, then cut six of the halves into four wedges (24 wedges altogether). Place four wedges on each marzipan tart base to form a square. Spoon 1 tablespoon of blackcurrants and ½ tablespoons of cassis coulis into the centre of each pie base. Place a halved plum on top of the purée. Whisk together the egg yolks and cream and use to brush a light coating around the edge of the pie base. Position the pastry lids on top and seal them to the base, using the prongs of a small fork to crimp the edges. Brush the top of each pie with the egg and cream mix, which will create a nice golden colour when baked. Bake the pies for 12–15 minutes or until golden. Allow to rest for 5 minutes before removing from the pastry rings. Serve hot with a scoop of the egg nog ice cream and the remaining cassis coulis in a jug on the side.

SERVES 6

HAZELNUT TIRAMISU TOWERS

This dessert is always a winner. It may be made in one large serving dish for a more family-oriented presentation. However, individual servings as presented in this recipe are a spectacular way of concluding a dinner.

300ml fresh espresso
2 tbsp cognac
4 tbsp Nutella spread
5 egg yolks
200g caster sugar
400g mascarpone
5 leaves gelatine
350ml cream
45 Savoiardi biscuits *(lady-fingers)*

tiramisu

Line the tubes in which the tiramisu will be built with a roll of acetate. Place the tubes on a tray lined with greaseproof paper and set aside until required. Pour the espresso coffee into a shallow, flat-bottomed bowl. Add the cognac and Nutella, mix together and allow the temperature to reduce to room temperature. In a separate bowl, whisk together the egg yolks and caster sugar until thick and creamy. Fold in the mascarpone. Cover the gelatine leaves in cold water and soak for 3 minutes. Heat 100ml of the cream in a small saucepan until simmering. Remove from the heat and add the softened gelatine leaves and stir until dissolved. Pour into the egg and mascarpone mixture. Whisk the remaining cream to soft peaks and fold into the egg, mascarpone and cream mixture. Dip and soak all of the Savoiardi biscuits in the espresso until they absorb the liquid, then remove and gently squeeze out almost all the liquid, leaving them just moist (too much espresso will turn them into a soggy mess). Prepare a tray lined with greaseproof paper that will fit into the freezer. Place a pastry cutter slightly smaller than the tubes in which the towers will be constructed on the tray, and fill the cutter to a depth of about 4mm with the soaked biscuits; they should be soft enough to be easily worked into the cutter shape. Remove the pastry cutter and repeat the process to make 30 discs. Place the tray with the discs in the freezer for 1 hour until they become quite hard, which will make it a lot easier to prepare the tiramisu towers. When hard, remove six discs from the tray and place one at the bottom of each tube. Spoon a layer of egg and mascarpone mixture across the Savoiardi disc. Use about one-fifth of the mascarpone mix between the six tubes. Place another disc on top of the mascarpone mix and continue making alternating layers until there are five layers of each. Refrigerate overnight — or for up to three days — before serving.

SIMON SAYS *When making the discs, be aware they will expand as they freeze so make them slightly smaller than the tube into which they must go. If some of the discs do not look dark enough, spoon a few more drops of espresso mix over them.*

2 tbsp grated dark chocolate
1 tbsp coffee balsamic mousse *(optional)*
6 strips candied vanilla bean *(see page 230)*
6 caramel tuiles *(see page 233)*

special equipment *6 x 75mm long tubes, each 55mm in diameter, acetate or overhead transparency film (readily available from stationery shops)*

assembly

Sift some grated chocolate on top of each tower. Position the towers on serving plates and remove the tubes. Using a pastry brush, paint a streak of coffee balsamic mousse on each plate and garnish with a candied vanilla bean and a tuile.

SERVES 6

WARM WALNUT CLAFOUTIS WITH STRAWBERRIES & COTTAGE CHEESE SORBET

Clafoutis is a French custard-style dessert typically made with cherries and baked in a batter similar to a pancake mixture. The walnut flour and walnut halves, along with the strawberries and cottage cheese sorbet on the side, make this a very pleasant dessert. The choice of soft fruit can be varied to suit seasonal availability or personal preference.

walnut clafoutis

2 medium eggs
2 egg yolks
250g unsalted butter, *melted*
100g caster sugar
70g walnut flour *(see page 234)*
10g plain flour

Combine the eggs, egg yolks and melted butter in a stainless mixing bowl and mix well. Sieve the sugar, walnut flour and plain flour into the egg and butter mix while stirring with a wooden spoon. Allow the batter to rest for a minimum of 2 hours.

cottage cheese sorbet

300ml still mineral water
100g caster sugar
250g cottage cheese

Combine the mineral water and sugar in a small saucepan and bring to the boil, then allow to cool. Process the cottage cheese and the sugar syrup in a blender until smooth. Pour into an ice cream machine or Pacojet and follow the manufacturer's instructions. Alternatively, freeze the sorbet in a suitable container, then remove and break into chunks and blend in a food processor until smooth before re-freezing.

assembly

16 strawberries
20 walnut halves

Preheat the oven to 180°C. Divide the clafoutis mixture evenly between four ovenproof serving dishes not filling them completely to allow a small amount of space for the clafoutis to rise. Arrange four strawberries and five walnut halves on the top of each dish. Bake for 10 minutes. Before serving, use a warmed ice cream scoop to place a serving of the cottage cheese sorbet in side dishes alongside.

SERVES 4

SPANISH BLUE CIGAR WITH MANUKA HONEY

This is a really unusual cheese presentation, which — provided no attempt is made to light them up and smoke them — should prove to be a considerable success.

75g Parmigiano-Reggiano, *grated*
50g Spanish Picón blue cheese or
   Gorgonzola Piccante
5 tsp manuka honey
1 tsp truffle oil

Divide the Parmigiano-Reggiano into five equal servings. Working with one serving at a time, spread each serving of cheese into an 8cm circle on a small flat plate. Microwave on high power for 30–40 seconds; watch carefully, as the cooking time will vary depending on the microwave's power. As soon as the cheese melts and starts to bubble, remove the plate from the microwave and immediately place one-fifth of the blue cheese in the centre, along with 1 teaspoon of honey and a couple of drops of truffle oil. Working as quickly as possible, roll up the melted cheese to form a cigar shape. Serve with a favourite port.

SIMON SAYS *Once the cheese has bubbled and is removed from the microwave, it needs to be handled quickly before it hardens and becomes difficult to roll.*

SERVES 5

GORGONZOLA DOLCE IN A CHAR-GRILLED PARMIGIANO CRÊPE WITH HOT ORANGE MARMALADE

It is believed by some that if you hold a piece of gold in your right hand and toss a crêpe and catch it in the pan with your left hand, you will become rich that year. I can state that quite the reverse is true; in fact, I am considerably out of pocket from having to have my kitchen floor cleaned so frequently, therefore I strongly advise against attempting this get-rich-quick scheme.

crêpes

50g plain flour
1 tsp caster sugar
¼ tsp flaky salt
1 egg
10 mlPukara extra-virgin olive oil
150ml milk
2 tbsp chopped chives
1 tbsp finely grated Parmigiano-Reggiano
olive oil spray

Sieve the flour, sugar and salt into a mixing bowl. Push the dry ingredients to one side of the bowl and add the egg to the other side, followed by the oil and milk. Gently mix together and then slowly incorporate the dry ingredients with a whisk (incorporating the dry ingredients slowly will avoid any lumps in the crêpe batter). Pass the batter through a sieve to ensure there are no lumps, then add the chives and grated Parmigiano. Mix well, then leave the batter to stand for 30 minutes to allow it to thicken. Heat a non-stick crêpe pan, then give it a light spray with the oil. Pour in 25ml of the batter and swirl it around in the pan to form a thin crêpe. Cook without colouring it for approximately 50 seconds, then flip the crêpe with a spatula to cook the other side. Transfer to a plate. Repeat until all the batter is used, which should result in 8-10 crêpes.

sauce

1 cup fresh orange juice
2 tbsp caster sugar

Combine the orange juice and sugar in a saucepan and bring to the boil. Reduce by three-quarters over a medium to high heat; this should take approximately 6–8 minutes. Once reduced, there will be approximately quarter of a cup of sauce. Place to one side until required.

assembly

olive oil spray
210g Gorgonzola Dolce
6 tsp orange and onion salsa *(see page 239 Salsarancia Cipolle)*
orange or mandarin balsamic mousse

Heat the grill or barbecue until smoking hot. Lightly coat the six crêpes with some oil spray and place on the grill for a few seconds, just enough so the char lines are visible. Divide the Gorgonzola into six equal portions and place a portion on each crêpe. Gently mould the crêpes into baskets. Place one on each serving plate, and spoon 1 teaspoon of the salsa next to it. Spoon a little orange sauce onto the plate and garnish with the balsamic mousse.

SERVES 6

BUILDING BLOCKS

anglaise

65g caster sugar
5 large egg yolks
1 vanilla bean or 1 tsp vanilla essence
1 cup cream
1 cup milk

In a bowl, whisk together the sugar and egg yolks until well blended. Using a sharp knife, split the vanilla bean down the centre and scrape the seeds into a small saucepan. Pour in the cream and milk, add the vanilla pod and bring to just below the boil over a medium heat. Remove from the heat and lift out the vanilla pod, setting it aside to use again. Whisk 2–3 tablespoons of the cream and milk mixture into the yolks. Gradually add the rest, whisking continuously. Pour into a bowl and position over a bain-marie. Gently heat the mixture to 77°C, stirring continuously with a wooden spoon. Do not allow the mixture to boil or the egg will scramble. Check for the desired consistency by coating the back of a spoon and running a finger through the centre of the coating; if the mixture does not run back together the thickening is complete. Immediately remove from the heat and pour the anglaise through a sieve. For maximum flavour, return the vanilla pod to the anglaise until it is required.

brioche

This recipe comes from Rob Burns, one of New Zealand's top bakers.

60g tepid milk
40g tepid water
10g fresh yeast
200g plain flour
pinch of salt
80g butter, *cubed*

Preheat the oven to 170°C. Place the milk, water, yeast, flour and salt in a mixing bowl and, using a dough hook, mix at slow speed for 1 minute until all the ingredients have combined. Increase the speed to medium and mix for 8 minutes, until the gluten structure has formed. Reduce the mixing speed to slow and add the butter gradually until well combined. When it is ready, the dough will look shiny and smooth. Turn out the dough and cut into 60g portions. Place the portions in prepared baking tins and set aside in a warm, draught-free spot to prove. The dough must reach just under the top of the tins before it is ready to bake. Bake for 20 minutes or until golden brown.

candied vanilla bean

1 vanilla bean
½ cup caster sugar
½ cup chilled water

Wash the vanilla bean well under cold running water. Using a sharp-pointed vegetable knife, split the vanilla bean lengthways into six very thin strips. Set aside. In a saucepan, bring the sugar and chilled water to a gentle simmer to make a simple sugar syrup. Reduce the heat to low, add the vanilla bean strips and simmer for 10 minutes, before allowing the strips to cool in the syrup. Carefully remove when cool, draining off any excess syrup. Place on a lined baking tray and dry in a low (120°C) oven for 2 hours until dry and crisp.

caramel wafers

½ cup caster sugar
1 tbsp corn syrup or liquid glucose
2 tbsp cold water

Combine the ingredients in a saucepan and bring to a gentle simmer over a moderate heat for a few minutes, giving the contents a very gentle swirl every minute or so. (As a general rule, sugar mixtures should not be stirred as this will cause the mix to crystallise.) Continue to gently simmer the sugar mix until it turns a light golden caramel colour and reaches 160°C on a sugar thermometer.

Remove from the heat to prevent further browning, then pour the mixture onto a lined tray and set aside to cool and set. Once cool, break it into small pieces and transfer to a food processor. Process to a fine crumb. Sprinkle the resulting caramel crumb onto the tray used earlier, using a template if desired to create an interesting shape. Increase the oven temperature to 180°C and bake the wafers for 3–4 minutes or until the caramel softens and melts. Remove from the oven and leave to stand for 1 minute before using a spatula to carefully lift the wafers from the paper, immediately draping them over a glass or rolling pin to introduce a curve as the shape sets.

Note: Take great care when working with hot sugar; it can cause serious burns.

chicken stock

2kg chicken bones
4 litres water
½ kg vegetables *(e.g. onion, carrot, celery, leek)*
100ml dry white wine
1 sprig of fresh thyme, or 1 tsp dried thyme
3 bay leaves
1 small bunch parsley
10 black peppercorns

Chop the bones and place in a saucepan. Cover the bones with cold water and bring to the boil. Drain off and rinse the bones under cold water. Clean the pot and put the bones back in, along with the 4 litres of water. Peel and roughly chop the vegetables and add to the pot along with the wine, thyme, bay leaves, parsley and black peppercorns. Bring to the boil, and simmer for 6 hours. The stock will evaporate so after 1 hour add another ½ litre of hot water. Skim the fat off the top and strain. Allow to cool. Divide into zip-lock bags, measuring the amount that goes into each bag and write this on the bag. Refrigerate or freeze.

chilli grape jam

160g green grapes, *halved and deseeded*
30ml water
30g sugar
12g port wine jelly
¼ tsp fresh red chilli, *finely chopped*
½ tsp grated fresh ginger

Place the grapes in a small saucepan with the water, sugar and port wine jelly. Bring the mixture to the boil, then simmer, stirring continuously, for 5 minutes until the liquid has reduced and is thick and glossy. Remove from the heat and add the chilli and ginger. Refrigerate in an airtight container until ready to use.

chocolate tuiles

125g caster sugar
60g glucose
45g dark chocolate

Preheat the oven to 180°C. Place the sugar and glucose into a clean saucepan over a medium heat and cook until the sugar reaches 160°C. Remove from the heat, add the chocolate and stir into the sugar mix. While the mixture is still hot, pour it onto a Silpat or Teflon sheet and set aside to cool and set. Once cool, break into small pieces and transfer to a food processor. Process to fine crumbs. Sprinkle the resulting crumb onto the tray used earlier, using a template if desired to create an interesting shape. Increase the oven temperature to 180°C and bake the wafers for 3–4 minutes or until the crumbs soften and melt. Remove from the oven and allow to cool. Once firm, store in an airtight container until required.

croutons

Remove the crusts from slices of toast bread and cut into cubes. Toss the cubes in a neutral oil and bake in a single layer on baking paper in a 200°C oven until golden and crisp.

Weigh the crusted bread to achieve the weight required or prepare the number needed according to the recipe being used. Store in an air-tight container.

fish stock

50ml Pukara extra-virgin olive oil
200g onions, sliced
2kg fish bones *(well washed)*
4 litres water
100ml dry white wine
juice of ½ lemon
5 parsley stalks
4 white peppercorns

If you cook this stock for longer than 20 minutes, the flavour will be bitter and the stock spoiled. Place the oil in a saucepan with the onions and fish bones. Cook on a low heat for 5 minutes, then add all remaining ingredients and bring to the boil. Simmer for 20 minutes. Remove from the heat, skim the fat off the top, strain and allow to cool. Divide into zip-lock bags, measuring the amount that goes into each bag and write this on the bag. Refrigerate or freeze.

gnocchi

3 large baking potatoes (about 780g)
1 large egg
1 tsp salt
¼ tsp freshly ground white pepper
pinch freshly grated nutmeg
2 cups unbleached all-purpose flour, or as needed

Bake the potatoes in a 220°C oven. When cooked and still as hot as can be handled, scrape the potato out of the skins into a bowl. Pass the scooped potato through a ricer and spread on a cool surface to allow to completely cool. Beat the egg, salt, pepper and nutmeg.

Bring the cooled potato together and make an indentation in the centre and pour in the egg mixture. Knead the potato and egg together, gradually adding the flour. Use only enough to form a smooth but slightly sticky dough.

The aim is to knead as little as possible in order to achieve a light dumpling.

Divide the dough into manageable pieces and pat (rather than roll) into ropes about a centimetre in diameter. Cut the ropes into individual dumpling lengths appropriate to the intended use. Take each dumpling and nestle it in the palm of one hand and then use the tines of a fork to create a ridged surface on the upper side of the dumpling. The lower side should be rounded as it is pressed into the palm.

Cook the formed dumplings immediately in lightly salted, vigorously boiling water. Cook only as many at a time as will fit into the container without sticking together. Cook until they rise to the surface and then for one further minute.

herb rub

20g fresh oregano
20g fresh thyme
20g dried basil
1 tsp salt
1 tsp cracked pepper

If you are not lucky enough to have found Simon Gault's Italian Herb Rub then make your own. Finely chop the oregano, thyme and basil and mix with the salt and pepper.

how to kill a crayfish

To kill a crayfish quickly and painlessly, place it on a cutting board, positioned so that the tail curls towards the board. Flatten it out as much as possible, then with one hand grasp the tail where it joins the body. Holding a large kitchen knife in the other hand, position the point between the eyes, with the blade facing away from the hand holding the tail. Press the point of the knife into the head, pressing firmly until it goes right through the crayfish's head and through to the cutting board, then bring the blade down firmly between the eyes. Drowning it is another option: place the crayfish in cold fresh water for about 30 minutes, but be warned that it's advisable to have a lid close at hand and you'll probably need to wear a raincoat. Never put a live crayfish into boiling water.

madeira jus
2kg beef bones with no fat (get your butcher to chop into small pieces)
50ml Pukara extra-virgin olive oil
1 large onion
1 large carrot
4 celery stalks
1 large leek
1 tbsp tomato paste
4 litres water
small bunch parsley stalks
10 black peppercorns
400ml Madeira
1 tbsp redcurrant jelly

Preheat the oven to 200°C. Place the bones in a roasting tray and roast in the oven for about 40 minutes or until the bones are brown. Remove from the oven and drain off any fat. In a fry pan heat the oil until shimmering. Add the vegetables and sauté for 4 minutes, then add the tomato paste. Remove the vegetables and place into a large stock-pot with water. Add the bones, parsley and peppercorns. Bring to the boil, skim off any fat and simmer for 6 hours. The stock will evaporate, so after 1 hour add another ½ litre of hot water. Remove from the heat and strain. Place the Madeira and redcurrant jelly in a clean saucepan, and bring to the boil. Add the stock and simmer until a silky smooth, almost gelatinous, sauce consistency is reached. Allow to cool. The sauce can be kept in the refrigerator for 5 days, or can be frozen in zip-lock bags.

mashed potato
2kg Agria potatoes
100g butter, cubed
125ml milk, hot
125ml cream, hot
1 pinch nutmeg
2 tbsp chopped parsley or chives
salt and pepper to taste
½ tbsp white truffle oil (optional)

In a saucepan, cover the potatoes with cold salted water and bring to the boil. Simmer until just past tender. Drain and pass through a potato ricer or mash with a potato masher. Add the butter to the hot milk and cream. Return the mashed potato to the heat and add the milk, cream and butter and stir until the mixture is smooth and creamy (all of the liquid may not be needed, depending on how starchy the potatoes are). Add the nutmeg and chopped herbs and season to taste. If you decide on the luxury of truffle oil, add it just before serving, with a final whisk.

mayonnaise
10ml malt vinegar
1 tbsp lemon juice
50ml water
1 tsp Lea & Perrins sauce
½ tbsp Colman's mustard powder
½ tbsp caster sugar
½ tbsp salt
4 egg yolks
950ml canola oil

Combine the vinegar, lemon juice, water and Lea & Perrins sauce in a pouring jug. Place the mustard, sugar, salt and yolks in mixer bowl with a whisk. Whisk on high speed for 30 seconds. Slowly trickle the oil onto the yolk mixture whilst on a medium speed, being careful not to add the oil too quickly as that will split the mayonnaise. After half the oil is added, add half the vinegar and lemon juice mixture, then continue adding oil. Once all the oil has been added, add the remaining vinegar and lemon juice mixture. The mayonnaise may be stored in the refrigerator in an airtight container for up to 3 months.

orange wafer
1 orange
1 tbsp caster sugar

Preheat the oven to 100°C. Using a very sharp knife or meat slicer, slice the orange so thinly that the slices are transparent. Remove any pips. Lay out about eight slices on a flat chopping board and sprinkle one side with the caster sugar. Cut each slice in half then, using tongs, transfer the slices to a Teflon or a non-stick sheet and bake for 1 hour or until dried. Remove the slices from the sheet and allow them to cool on a flat surface. Store in an airtight container until required.

MAKES 8

oven-roasted tomatoes
Preheat the oven to 220°C. Prick the tomatoes three times around the calyx (where the tomato was attached to the vine), just breaking the skin. Place on an oiled oven tray and roast until the skin begins to blister and blacken (about 15 minutes).

simple sugar syrup
1 level cup caster sugar
2 cups water

Combine the sugar and water in a saucepan and heat until the sugar dissolves; don't allow it to boil. Allow to cool, then set aside until required. It will keep for up to 2 weeks.

sweet and spicy rub
60g white sugar
20g brown sugar
15g paprika
½ tsp cayenne pepper
15g plain salt

Mix together.

tempura batter (1)
175ml ice-cold soda water
1 egg
9 tbsp tempura flour, *chilled*

Combine the water and egg in a bowl. Mix well with a fork then add the flour. Still using the fork, mix the flour and liquid together, ensuring that little bubbles of flour remain evenly distributed through the batter. During cooking, these bubbles expand and disintegrate, creating lightness and assisting in the crispness. The batter will look a little thin compared to normal batters, but this is to be expected.

tempura batter using Trisol (2)
175ml ice-cold soda water
3 tbsp Trisol
6 tbsp tempura flour, *chilled*

Dissolve the Trisol in the water. Pour the mixture over the tempura flour and whisk until combined.

SIMON SAYS *It is important to have all the ingredients chilled, including the flour; this assists in making the batter crisp.*

MAKES 225ML

tomato concasse
To make tomato concasse (*concasse* is French for a coarsely chopped mixture), first skin the tomatoes. Cut a cross in the base of each tomato, then place them in boiling water for about 1 minute or until the skin starts to peel away from the flesh. Transfer the tomatoes to a bowl of iced water, and when cool enough to handle, remove the skin and core, then cut each tomato in half, remove the seeds and chop the flesh into small dice. (I once worked in an English restaurant where the chef fined his staff £1 for every seed he found in their concasse.)

tomato sauce
50ml Pukara extra-virgin olive oil
3 medium cloves garlic, minced
½ white onion, *roughly chopped*
1 cup canned Italian whole peeled tomatoes
½ cup vegetable stock or chicken stock
½ tsp salt

Heat the olive oil in a saucepan until shimmering. Add the garlic and onion and sauté over a medium heat for about 7 minutes or until the onion is transparent. Take care not to burn the garlic. Add the tomatoes and simmer for 30 minutes. Process briefly in a blender until the correct texture is achieved. If the sauce is too thick, dilute with vegetable or chicken stock but be careful to consider how salty the stock may be. Add salt to taste.

tuiles
75g flour
75g icing sugar
75g egg whites
75g softened butter

Preheat the oven to 180°C. Sieve the flour and icing sugar into a bowl. Add the egg whites, working the mixture together to a smooth paste. Gradually incorporate the soft butter, mixing well. Allow the dough to rest in the refrigerator for at least 2 hours for best results. Using a Stanley knife or similar, cut a triangular-shaped template out of an ice cream container lid. Position the template on a Teflon sheet or baking tray, and using a palette knife, spread the mixture within the template to 2mm thick. Repeat to make desired number of tuiles. Bake the tuiles for 6 minutes or until lightly coloured. Remove from the oven and, while they are still hot, use the palette knife to lift them from the tray and drape them over a bottle or rolling pin (you might need to use more than one) to achieve the desired shape and leave to cool. Once firm, store in an airtight container until required.

SIMON SAYS *You can stir into the mixture prior to baking any of the following: cinnamon, ground ginger, grated orange zest or cocoa.*

vinaigrette
1½ tablespoons Colman's mustard powder
1 tbsp caster sugar
2 tsp salt
60ml water
670ml canola oil
335ml canola oil
335ml water
335ml olive oil
335ml malt vinegar

In a blender, place the mustard powder, sugar, salt and first measure of water. Blend for 20 seconds. Slowly dribble in the first measure of canola oil on a medium speed. Combine the second measure of canola oil and the second measure of water. Slowly dribble into

the blender. Combine the the olive oil and malt vinegar and dribble into the blender. Store in an airtight container in the fridge for up to 6 months. Shake before using.

walnut flour

Although it is possible to buy walnut flour in some specialty shops, you can make your own by processing ⅓ cup fresh walnuts until a fine flour-like powder is achieved. Mix with ½ cup plain flour, then pass through a sieve. Store in an airtight container.

using a Pacojet

SIMON SAYS *I use a Pacojet for all my ice cream and sorbet recipes. It is a breakthrough in food technology and I find it very useful — not just for sorbets and ice creams, but much more. If using an ice cream machine rather than a Pacojet to make any of the ice cream recipes in this book, be aware that the ice cream will be quite hard. This problem can be solved by removing the ice cream or sorbet from the freezer a short time before serving.*
www.wildfire.co.nz

egg nog ice cream

½ cup caster sugar
3 egg yolks
350ml milk
150ml cream
pinch of nutmeg
40ml bourbon

Whisk the sugar and egg yolks together in a bowl until pale. Combine the milk and cream in a saucepan and heat until just coming to the boil. Pour one-third of the hot milk and cream over the sugar and yolk mixture, whisking well. Add the remaining milk and cream to the bowl. Return the mixture to the saucepan and cook over a very low heat until the mixture reaches 85°C. Stirring constantly, add the nutmeg and bourbon; the alcohol will be evaporated by the heat. Pour the mixture into a Pacojet canister or ice cream machine and follow the manufacturer's instructions or pour into a freezer-safe container and place in the freezer, removing it to whisk every 20 minutes until frozen.

yoghurt sorbet

500g natural yoghurt
120g caster sugar
100ml cream
2 tbsp liquid glucose

In a bowl, whisk together the yoghurt, sugar, cream and glucose. Pour into a Pacojet canister or ice cream machine and follow the manufacturer's instructions.

GLOSSARY

Acetaia Malpighi white balsamic vinegar
Acetaia means vinegar factory. Malpighi is a family in Modena, Italy, who are fifth generation Balsamic vinegar makers.

aïoli [ay-OH-lee; I-OH-lee]
A strongly flavoured garlic mayonnaise from the Provence region of southern France. It's a popular accompaniment for fish, meats and vegetables.

Alaskan red king crab
Made famous by the *Discovery* programme, *The World Deadliest Catch*. There is no meat in the bodies, only in the leg claws. They are available from any good gourmet seafood store.

al dente [al-DEN-tay]
An Italian phrase meaning 'to the tooth', used to describe pasta or other food that is cooked until it offers a light resistance when bitten into, but is not soft or overdone.

Algin
A natural product extracted from brown algae of *Laminaria, Fucus and Macrocystis* genera, among others, that grow in cold-water regions off Ireland, Scotland, North and South America, Australia, New Zealand and South Africa. Depending on the part of the algae that has been refined, the texture and reactivity of each alginate varies. For this reason, we have selected Texturas Algin as the ideal product for achieving spherification with guaranteed results. Visit *www.souschef.co.nz*

arborio rice [ar-BOH-ree-oh]
The high-starch kernels of this Italian-grown grain are shorter and fatter than any other short-grain rice. Arborio is traditionally used for risotto because the high starch lends this classic dish its requisite creamy texture.

arugula [ah-ROO-guh-lah]
Also known as Italian cress, rocket, roquette, rugula and rucola, arugula is a bitterish, aromatic salad green with a peppery mustard flavour.

bain-marie [bahn-ma-ree]
Hot water bath where a bowl is placed over a larger bowl or saucepan of simmering water. Used to melt ingredients or to provide slow, even cooking.

balsamic vinegar [bal-SAH-mic]
Exquisite Italian vinegar made from white Trebbiano grape juice. It gets its dark colour and pungent sweetness from aging in barrels — of various woods and in graduating sizes — over a period of years. Many balsamic vinegars contain sulphites, which are primarily added to inhibit the growth of unfavourable, flavour-detracting bacteria.

Saporoso balsamic vinegar
An aged (six years) balsamic vinegar produced by Acetaia Malpighi in Modena, Italy.

balsamusse
A trade name for the balsamic mousse produced by Antica Balsameria Emiliana.

barley
This hardy grain dates back to the Stone Age and has been used throughout eons in dishes ranging from cereals to breads to soups (such as the famous Scotch broth). Most of the barley grown in the Western world is used either for animal fodder or, when malted, to make beer and whisky.

bluff oyster
Bluff oysters are the most valuable species found in New Zealand that are not yet farmed. They are grown slowly in the cold, clean waters of Foveaux Strait and in season are dredged by the Bluff oyster fleet

brunoise [broo-NWAHZ]
A mixture, normally of vegetables, that has been very finely diced.

bruschetta [broo-SKEH-tah]
From the Italian *bruscare* meaning 'to roast over coals', this traditional garlic bread is made by rubbing slices of toasted bread with garlic cloves, then drizzling the bread with extra-virgin olive oil. The bread is salted and peppered, then heated and served warm.

buffalo mozzarella [moz-zuh-REHL-lah]
Hailing from Italy, this is a mild, white fresh cheese. Buffalo mozzarella is the most prized of the fresh mozzarellas. It is made from water buffalo milk.

calamari [kah-ul-MAHR-ee]
Also called squid. The meat has a firm texture and mild, somewhat sweet flavour.

Calcic
This product is a calcium salt traditionally used in the food industry, for example in cheese making. Calcic is essential in the reaction with Texturas Algin that produces spherification. It is the ideal reactant for its high water solubility, considerable calcium content, and consequently great capacity for producing spherification. Visit *www.souschef.co.nz*

canola oil
The market name for rapeseed oil, which

comes from rapeseeds. It is the lowest of all the oils in saturated fats, and only olive oil has more monounsaturated fats. (Saturated fats increase 'bad' or LDL cholesterol levels as well as total cholesterol levels. Monounsaturated fats decrease the level of both total and 'bad' cholesterol, and increase the level of 'good' or HDL cholesterol. Polyunsaturated fats decrease 'bad' cholesterol and maintain the level of 'good' cholesterol.)

capers
The flower bud of a bush native to the Mediterranean and parts of Asia. The small buds are picked, sun-dried and then salted or pickled in a vinegar brine.

carpaccio [kahr-pah-chee-oh]
Italian in origin, carpaccio consists of thin shavings of raw beef, fish, vegetables or fruits which may be drizzled with olive oil and lemon juice.

chervil
A mild-flavoured herb, and a member of the parsley family. This aromatic herb has curly, dark green leaves with a slight anise flavour.

cipoline onion [chip-oh-lee-nay]
A small, flat, pale, sweet onion with higher residual sugar than regular onions, often purchased in jars or cans with oil or balsamic vinegar. Ideal for antipasto platters or with boiled meats.

Citras
A product made from sodium citrate, obtained mainly from citrus. It is usually used in the food industry to prevent the darkening of cut fruits and vegetables. It reduces the acidity of foods, and using it makes it possible to achieve spherical preparations with strongly acidic ingredients. It dissolves easily and acts instantaneously. Visit *www.souschef. co.nz*

concasse
Concasse is French for a coarsely chopped mixture.

coriander
A herb related to the parsley family, native to the Mediterranean and the Orient. The leaves have an extremely pungent odour and flavour.

crème fraîche [krehm FRESH]
This is a matured, thickened cream, which has a slightly tangy, nutty flavour and velvety, rich texture.

crêpe [KREHP]
The French word for 'pancake', which is exactly what these light, paper-thin creations are.

crostini [kroh-stee-nee]
Small thin slices of toasted bread.

dariole [dah-ree-OHL]
A French term referring to a small, cylindrical mould, as well as to the dessert baked in it.

flour 00
The Italians use zeroes to indicate how finely flour is ground. Tipo 0 is not as finely ground as Tipo 00. Note also that Tipo 00 can have further categories: 00 pizza and 00 pastry. Further, the 00 pastry flours have different characteristics which suit different baking needs.

gazpacho [gahz-PAH-choh]
A refreshingly cold summertime soup hailing from the Andalusia region in southern Spain.

gelatine [JEHL-ul-tihn]
An odourless, tasteless and colourless thickening agent which, when dissolved in water, forms a jelly.

Gellan
A recently discovered gelling agent obtained from the fermentation of *Sphingomonas elodea* bacteria. Gellan allows chefs to obtain a firm gel that slices cleanly and withstands temperatures of 90°C. Visit *www.souschef.co.nz*

gorgonzola dolce [gohr-guhn-SOH-lah DOHL-chay]
Also called *dolcelatte*, this soft, mild, blue-veined cheese can be served as either an appetiser or dessert.

Gluco
A mixture of two calcium salts that is perfect for inverse spherification but adds no flavour to the food.

inverse spherification
Allows jellification, as in basic spherification, but with products high in natural calcium and not suited to basic spherification.

julienne
Foods that have been cut into thin, matchstick strips.

Lecite
A natural soy lecithin-based emulsifier used to produce stable foams.

Manchego [mahn-CHAY-goh]
Spain's most famous cheese, named because it was originally made only from the milk of Manchego sheep. It is a rich, golden, semi-firm cheese that has a full, mellow flavour.

mascarpone [mahs-kahr-POH-nay]
Hailing from Italy's Lombardy region, mascarpone is a buttery-rich double-cream to triple-cream cheese made from cow's milk. It is ivory-coloured, soft and delicate.

Murray River sea salt
A natural Australian inland salt from the Murray Darling basin. Pinkish to apricot in colour and containing naturally occurring minerals.

osciètre caviar
This elegant and expensive fish roe from the sturgeon is considered the true caviar. Traditionally from the Caspian Sea, it is now farmed in France and Germany.

Pacojet
A breakthrough in food processing technology which allows deep-frozen foodstuffs to be mixed and puréed without being thawed first.

palette knife
A blunt knife with an extremely flexible steel blade ideal for spreading icing or other mixtures and for loosening cakes and other baked items from the tin.

Parmigiano-Reggiano [pahr-muh-ZHAH-noh reh-zhee-AH-noh]
This Italian hard, dry cheese is made from skimmed or partially skimmed cow's milk. It has a hard, pale-golden rind and a straw-coloured interior with a rich, sharp flavour. Parmigiano-Reggiano should be aged for not less than 18 months.

Prelibato
A clear to golden vinegar made from the must of white grapes and aged in ash barrels. Use with fish, shellfish, fresh fruit and green salads.

prosciutto [proh-SHOO-toh]
Italian for 'ham', prosciutto (more correctly prosciutto crudo) is a term broadly used to describe a ham that has been seasoned, salt-cured (but not smoked) and air-dried. The meat is pressed, which produces a firm, dense texture. Italy's Parma ham Prosciutto di Parma is the true prosciutto.

ratatouille [ra-tuh-TOO-ee]
A popular dish from the French region of Provence that combines eggplant, tomatoes, onions, capsicums, courgettes, garlic and herbs — all sautéed in olive oil. It can be served hot or cold, either as a side dish or as an appetizer with bread or crackers.

reduce
To boil a liquid (usually stock, wine or a sauce mixture) rapidly until the volume is reduced by evaporation, thereby thickening the consistency and intensifying the flavour.

ricotta [rih-KAHT-tuh]
This rich, fresh cheese is slightly grainy but smoother than cottage cheese, is moist and has a slightly sweet flavour. Most Italian ricottas are made from the whey from the makings of such cheeses as mozzarella and provolone.

risotto [ree-ZAW-toh]
An Italian rice specialty made by stirring hot stock into a mixture of Arborio rice and chopped onions that have been sautéed in butter.

rotisserie [roh-TIS-uh-ree]
A unit that cooks food while it slowly rotates. This type of cooking allows heat to circulate evenly around the food while it self-bastes with its own juices.

saffron [SAF-ruhn]
The world's most expensive spice. It originates from the stigma of a small purple crocus flower.

sauté [saw-TAY]
To cook food quickly in a small amount of oil or other fat in a sauté pan over direct heat.

shimmering
Oil heated to a point where the surface begins to ripple but does not smoke.

shiso [SHEE-soh]
Aromatic green jagged leaf of the parilla plant which is part of the mint and basil family. The versatile green shiso is used in salads and sushi.

Silpat
The brand name of a popular silicone mat that can be used in place of baking paper and which provides a non-stick surface used in the production of confectionery.

sugar thermometer
A thermometer used to measure the temperature and therefore the stage of cooking of a sugar solution. It is similar to a meat thermometer except that it can read higher temperatures (usually 200°C or more).

tempering
A technique used to blend uncooked eggs into hot liquid or sauce. A small amount of the hot liquid is stirred into the eggs to warm (temper) them and slowly raise their temperature. The egg mixture is diluted without it scrambling.

Texturas tool kit
A set of tools designed specifically for working with the El Bulli Texturas range of products.

Trisol
An additive used with flour to improve the texture of batters and reduce oil absorbence during deep frying, produced by Solé Graells of Spain.

truffles
Some define them as the food of the

gods. Truffles are a rare and delicate type of edible mushroom that are grown mainly in Italy and France, and now Australia and New Zealand. Truffles grow underground among the roots of oak, elm, chestnut, hazelnut, pine and willow trees. Duplicating the right conditions for growing truffles commercially is not feasible or cost effective on a wide scale, hence their high price.

vanilla bean

These long, thick pods are the fruit of an orchid. They are available from supermarkets and most specialty food stores. To use vanilla beans, slit them lengthways down the centre and scrape out the thousands of seeds. These seeds can be added directly to foods. Whole pods that have been used to flavour sauces or other mixtures may be rinsed, dried and stored for reuse.

wasabi [WAH-sah-bee]

This Japanese version of horseradish comes from the root of an Asian plant. It is used to make a green-coloured condiment that has a sharp, pungent, fiery flavour.

wasabi tobiko caviar

Wasabi-infused flying-fish roe.

Whip-it

The brand name of a type of whipped cream dispenser.

whitebait

A tiny transparent fish, this New Zealand delicacy is caught in the lower reaches of rivers using small, open-mouthed, hand-held nets. New Zealand whitebait is small, sweet and tender, with a delicate taste.

All the products mentioned in the book are available from souschef. Visit www.souschef.co.nz

El Bulli Texturas Range

Simon Gault Italian Herb Rub

Pancetta

Serrano sliced jamon

Italian Mascarpone cheese

Sautéed Porcini Mushrooms

Mozzarella di Bufala

Manchego wheel

 Extra-Virgin Olive Oil

 Tartufalba white truffle oil

 Black Truffle Oil

 Santagata Extra-Virgin Olive Oil

 Chocolate Grappa Italy

 Chipotle Smoked Tabasco

 Jalapeño Green Tabasco

 White asparagus spears

 Artichokes with stem

 Semi-dried Tomatoes

 Olive Bella di Cerignola

 Cipolline Onions in Balsamic

 Saporitore

 Salle alle Erbe

 Saporitore alle Vongole

 Porcini Mushroom Stock

 Fumetto di Pesce

Anchovy fillets

 Salsarancia Cipolle

 Salsafragola

 Salsafichi

 Crema Con Tartufo

 Crema di Funghi Porcini

 Crema di Olive

 Salsa di Pomodori Verdi

 Salsa di Pomodori Secchi

 Prelibato White Balsamic

 Traditional Balsamic 12yr

 Saporoso Balsamic 6yr

 Digitech Scale (200 x 0.1gr)

ACKNOWLEDGEMENTS

In this book I have presented a collection of menu dishes and their associated recipes that I have used over several years, initially in my own restaurants and latterly in the restaurants that make up the Nourish Group. As a partner and in the role as executive chef for the Nourish Group I am responsible for menu creation and the standard of cuisine presented. But writing a menu, however good and imaginative it might be, isn't going to be worth a great deal without technically skilled and dedicated professionals who are able to translate the ideas and methods into plated magic. I want to recognise the contribution of every member of the Nourish team in whatever role because if ever there was an industry that required the ultimate in teamwork, it is the restaurant industry. I am immensely fortunate to have gathered a team whose passion for excellence is reflected in all that they do. It would not be possible to quantify their contribution toward the success of our restaurant group, but they have my admiration, respect and gratitude for their loyalty and the camaraderie that we share. Long-time friend Shane Yardley, head chef at Euro, deserves special mention as a brilliant contributor along with his team of Robert Hope-ede, William Blackmore, Nicolas Fiche, Bob Lun, Gerard Doran, Matai Kavana, Paul Povey, Di Liu, Tristan Edgerley, Gilles Goiran and Ben Smith, who tested many of these recipes after they were modified for the book. Thanks to Shed 5 restaurant head chef Glen Turner for his dedication to the restaurant's continued excellent rating and to his team Kristin (Flick) Hooper, Carl Maunder, Andrew Blow, Emma Hurst, Nicholas Barrand, Jeremy Bruce, Patrick Chapman, Tina Nguyen, Blayne Still and Khan Whitehouse, who were also involved in testing recipes. Others whom I wish to thank include Shed 5 fishmonger Richard Waru; Jacob Cable, kitchen porter for 14 years; Jason Bartley, head chef for Pravda, for his continued excellence, and his stalwart team of Daniel Paton and Matthew Jackson; Darren Lim, head chef at the Jervois Steak House, not forgetting his team of Kory Ashby, Lucas Currie and Christopher Field; my goddaughter and commis chef Daniele O'Brien; chef Eugene Hamilton, formerly head chef for Shed 5 and now my right-hand man and minder (Eugene and I go back many years — his technical skills are exceptional and his friendship and support are immensely important to me). Never far from the action has been Steven Overend whose ideas, innovative thinking, computer skills and sheer brilliance as a maître d' have had a hugely beneficial influence over many years. Thank you also to my partners and friends Richard Sigley, Phil Clark, Brian Fitzgerald and Anton Haagh for their support and confidence in my judgement and for making this book and many other things possible. Finally, thanks to Kieran Scott who brilliantly photographed my food, Karryn Muschamp for her excellent design, and Margaret Sinclair, my commissioning editor, for her support and incomprehensible patience.

I want also to thank the team at Sous Chef (Mike, Becs, Nathan, Fern and Bryan) who share the vision; it is their intuitive judgment that has enabled us to continually source the best of European products. As well I would like to acknowledge our loyal customers who have followed us over the many stages of our journey and who are, after all, our 'raison d'être'.

My achievements, disappointments and good and bad times have been felt and endured by my parents, Ellerie and Bryan, and my sister Sarah. My dad has probably spent as many hours assisting, advising and mentoring as he logged during his flying career. Without his assistance, this book would probably have been no more than an idea. At this time I believe it would be injurious to my health to suggest that we embark on a third book. It is the strength of our common effort and family bond that has ensured the journey has continued. Neglect seems to be an integral part of a chef's life, partly I think because it is incredibly difficult to arouse the interest of one's family in a social get-together after finishing work at 2a.m.

INDEX

A RANDOM HOUSE BOOK
published by Random House New Zealand
18 Poland Road, Glenfield, Auckland, New Zealand

For more information about our titles
go to www.randomhouse.co.nz

A catalogue record for this book is available from the
National Library of New Zealand

Random House International, Random House, 20 Vauxhall
Bridge Road, London, SW1V 2SA, United Kingdom; Random
House Australia Pty Ltd, Level 3, 100 Pacific Highway, North
Sydney 2060, Australia; Random House South Africa Pty Ltd,
Isle of Houghton, Corner Boundary Road and Carse O'Gowrie,
Houghton 2198, South Africa; Random House Publishers India
Private Ltd, 301 World Trade Tower, Hotel Intercontinental
Grand Complex, Barakhamba Lane, New Delhi 110 001, India

First published 2008
© 2008 text Simon Gault
© 2008 images Kieran Scott

The moral rights of the author have been asserted
ISBN 978 1 877408 10 6 (hardback)
ISBN 978 1 86979 050 9 (limp)

Design: Karryn Muschamp
Printed in China by South China Printing Co Ltd

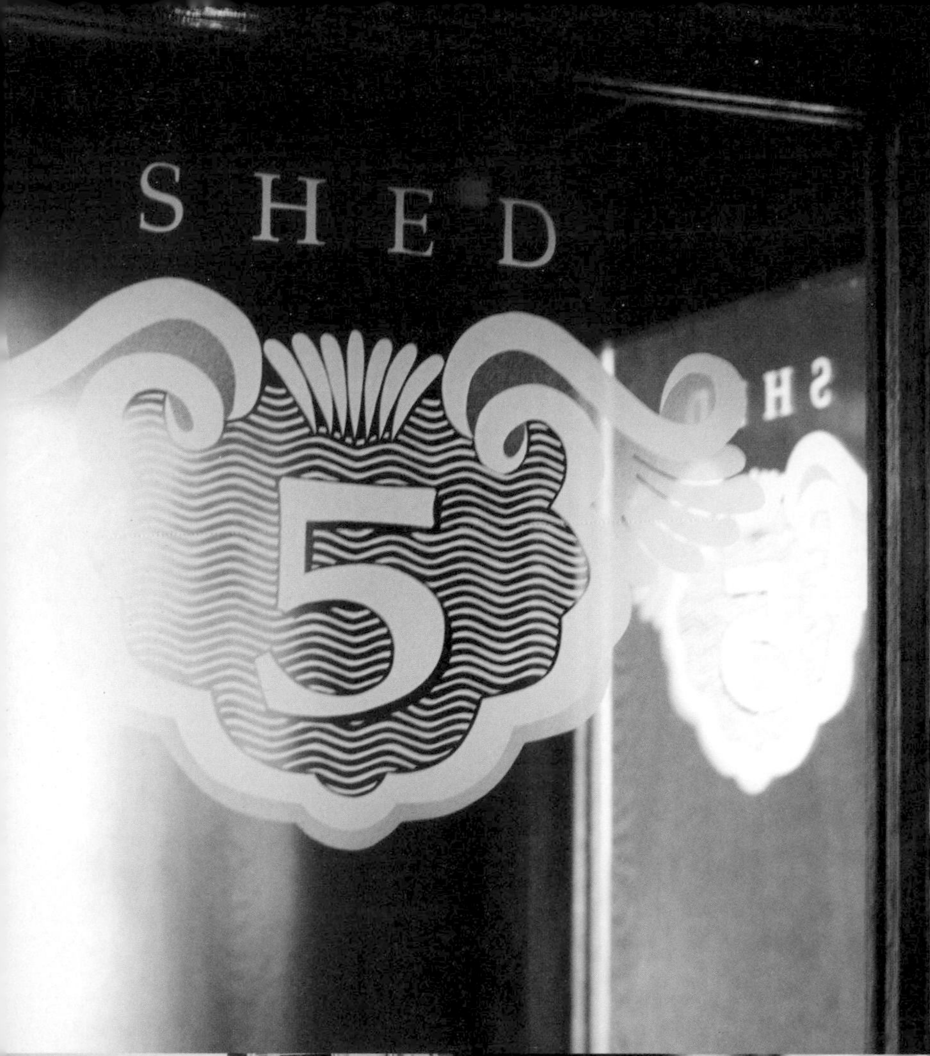
SHED
5
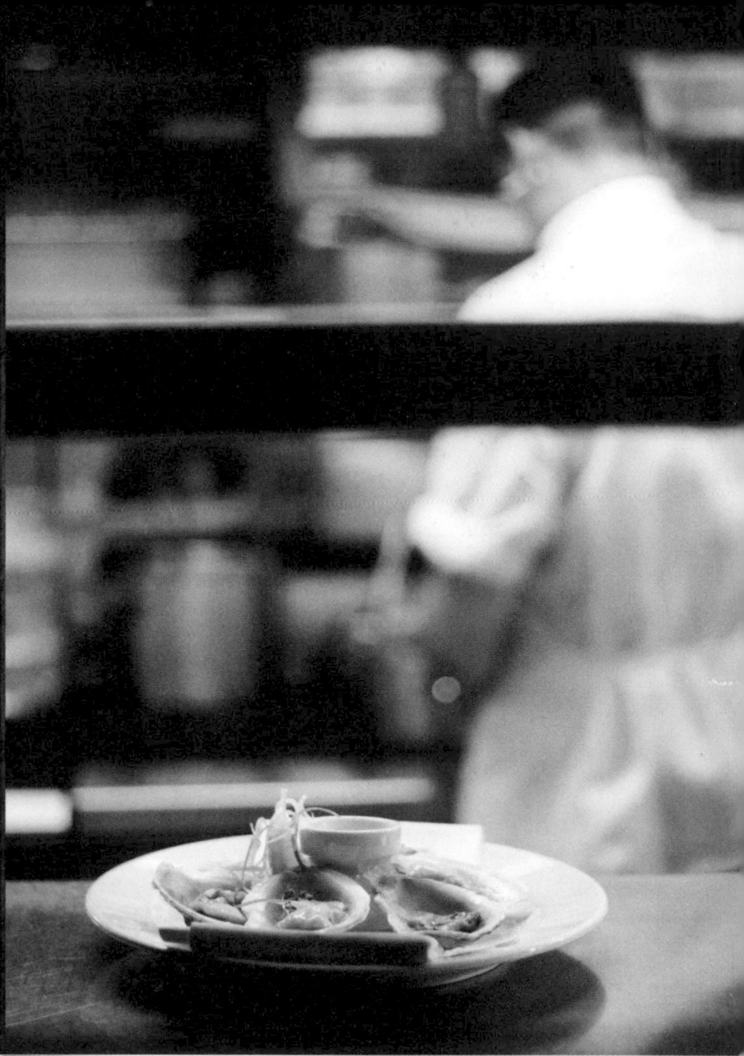
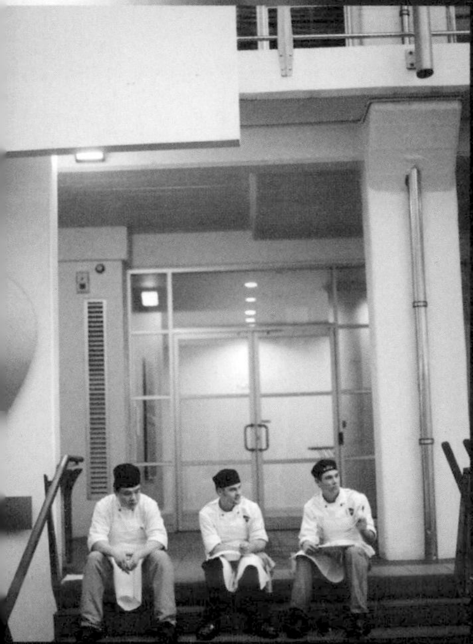
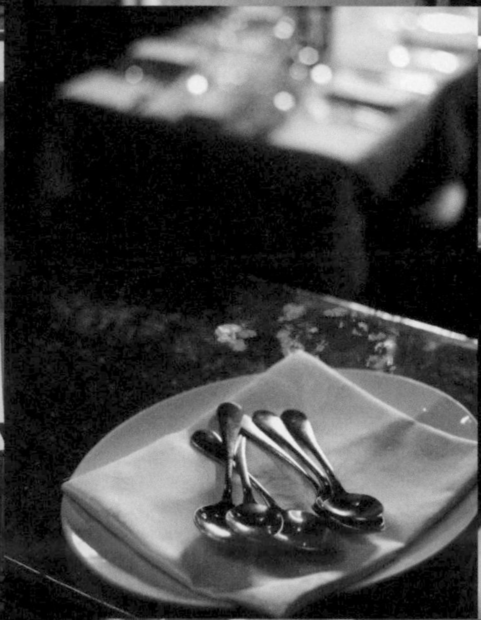
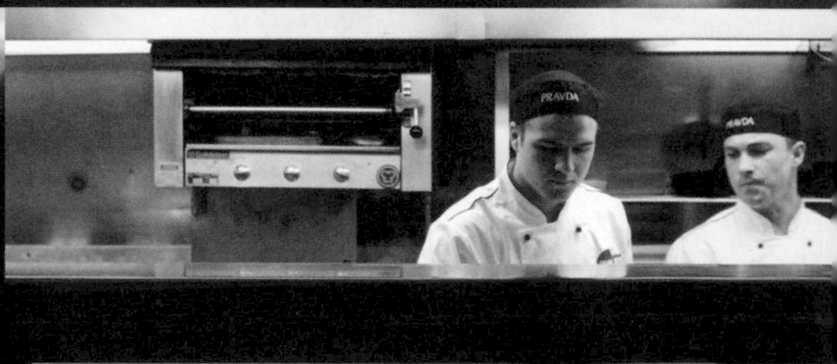
PRAVDA
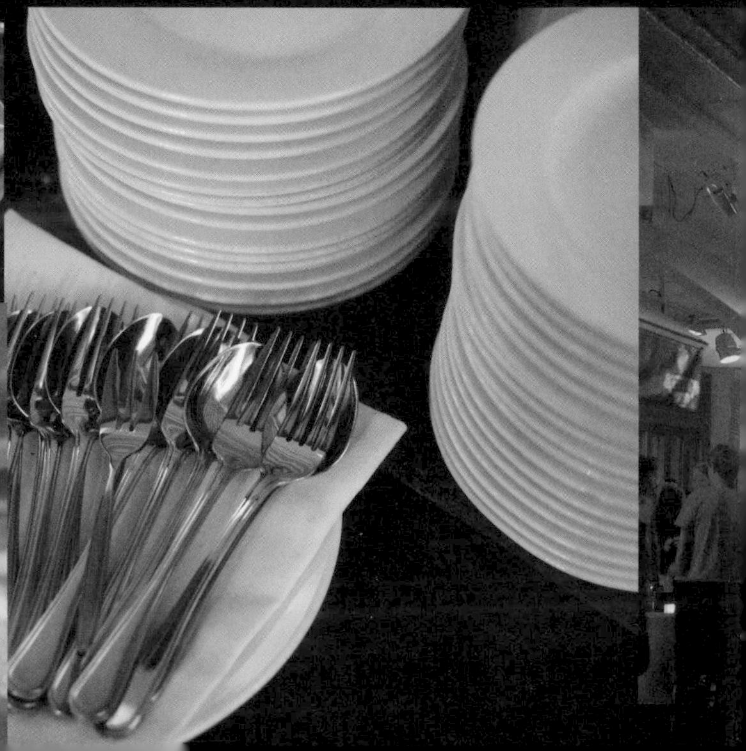
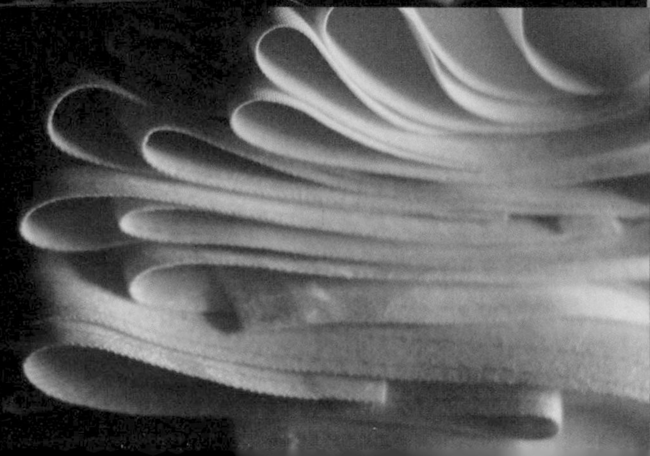